KARLA ANTOINETTE BAPTISTE

FOREWORD BY
KIM F. RHOADS, MD, MS, MPH, FACS
OF STANFORD UNIVERSITY

Dig in Your Heels

THE GLAMOROUS
(AND NOT SO GLAMOROUS)
LIFE OF A YOUNG
BREAST CANCER SURVIVOR

Antiste Publishing

Paperback ISBN: 978-0-578-16948-4
Hardback ISBN: 978-0-578-16949-1

Library of Congress Control Number: 2015951844

PRINTED IN THE UNITED STATES OF AMERICA

Dedication

*An African proverb says "It takes a village to raise
a child." Well, it also takes a village to get someone
through breast cancer. There was my primary doctor,
my breast surgeon, my plastic surgeon, my oncologist,
my radiologist, my nurses, my phlebotomists and
that's just the medical staff. Family, friends, colleagues,
and strangers prepared meals, drove me to chemo,
sent cards and gifts, and whispered prayers. This book
is dedicated to all of them--my village. I wouldn't be
where I am today without them.*

Table of Contents

Foreword

by

Kim F. Rhoads, M.D., M.S., M.P.H., F.A.C.S.

By sharing her story about love, trust, companionship, religious and spiritual faith, Karla Antoinette Baptiste takes us on a personal journey through pain, self-reflection, healing and existential triumph. They say when life gives you lemons, you make lemonade. In this story, life handed Karla onions and she has whipped up the tastiest batch of French onion soup (*soupe à l'oignon gratinée*, as she would call it), that anyone has ever consumed. *Dig in Your Heels* is easily digestible and keeps the reader coming back for more with humor, humility and a glimpse into a few great parties, both in Europe and here at home. The celebration of life is rooted in the storyline, in the commitment to (and from) her close knit family and Karla's no nonsense approach to the shenanigans of her off again, on again husband, Jamal. The story is real, feels alive and similar to the *Chicken Soup for the Soul* series, provides a warm bowl of *soupe à l'oignon gratinée*, for women and families affected by breast cancer.

Breast cancer impacted my family while I was a second year medical student. My favorite aunt, Jeannette Barnes, was diagnosed with late stage cancer. I came to really know my aunt Jeannette during the year between college and medical school after moving to the Washington D.C. Metro area. On lonely weekends, I would drive from Maryland to Norfolk, Virginia to visit my favorite cousins, my uncle "Pig" and my aunt Jeannette. My aunt Jeannette was my mom's older sister, confidant, chuckle buddy and bonded sister. She was short in stature but a giant in life force. During those visits, we would often chat about the health care system and how it might better cater to the needs of African Americans. I remember distinctly hearing Aunt Jeannette talk about wanting to receive care in a local setting where people knew her, would not judge her and would provide care to her as if she were family. She was looking for community.

By the time she was diagnosed, the tumor was so far advanced that it had erupted through the skin, outgrown its blood supply, and the tissue was starting to die. The tumor began to give off an odor and she could no longer hide it from the family. Suddenly the importance of her comments about wanting to be treated where she felt herself a part of a community made perfect sense to me. The tumor had been there all along, but she was concerned with what she might face inside the health care system—including the financial expense and the burden she imagined it would be on the family. She was prescribed a taxing course of chemotherapy and I was informed by the surgeon that she could never have an operation because the tumor was too large. On Christmas Eve of 1993, she died at the very young age of fifty-eight.

Over more than twenty years of medical training, my aunt Jeannette's story has served as a critical motivator for my work in cancer disparities, including and most importantly, my leadership and founding of Stanford Cancer Institute's Community Partnership Program (SCI-CPP) in 2010. In the summer of 2013, one of our programs called Sustainable Education for Eliminating Disparities in Breast Cancer (SEED)[1] trained its first cohort of community advocates, or "Ambassadors for Change"[2]. This is where I first met Karla. She was strikingly beautiful and her presence so effervescent. Had she not introduced herself as a survivor, we never would have guessed all that this young, fresh faced woman had been through.

The mission of the SEED program dictates that the trained Ambassadors take the information they gain through the training and put it into action: share and deliver it to other people in need. In her first book, *Dig in Your Heels*, Karla has realized this goal and more. Karla's memoir clearly explains how and why she would be involved in this way and emphasizes her importance and potential as a force in breast cancer advocacy.

I credit my aunt Jeannette's experience for propelling the development of my professional interests and accomplishments. But Karla's memoir gives legs to my own dream of helping others dig in their heels in the battle against breast cancer in a way that I was not prepared so early in my training to help my aunt. With this touching memoir, I know that women and families needing support will have a reliable and welcoming place to turn for information, inspiration and hope.

This book is for anyone who is going through breast cancer as a personal battle, as well as for those forming the communities that fight alongside the survivors. This book is for the

---

1   SEED is a project funded by the California Breast Cancer Research Program and the Stanford Cancer Institute.
2 ʼ   Ambassadors for Change is a concept developed by Pamela Ratliff, Copyright 2014

religious, the non-religious faithful and the atheist looking for something to believe in. This book is for every woman who believes that breast cancer is not a period, but a comma; the beginning of a new normal, with the best still yet to come. What Karla gives us all through the telling of her memoir, is reason to believe in the strength of the human spirit. While the book does not promise that everything will be 'okay' in every case, it is a strong reminder that everything will work out the way it is supposed to; but only if you put on your pumps, engage with the path on which you are walking and dig in your heels!

Introduction

I'm a breast cancer survivor who has done my share of breast cancer walks, and while they are festive and it doesn't hurt me to get the exercise, they just don't do it for me. One reason is that until recently I sucked at fundraising. My mother always sold my candy for school fundraisers when I was a kid. I did pretty well with raising funds for breast cancer walks when I was first diagnosed because people probably felt sorry for me. The next year? Not so much. I did two breast cancer walks in one year and I felt like people were thinking, "Is she going to hit us up every time there's one of these things?" Given my track record with fundraising at the time, I believed I could do more for breast cancer by telling my story than I could if I participated in a walk/race. Therefore, a couple of years after my diagnosis, I started writing this book. Ironically, I had to raise the funds to publish it and, to my surprise, I received a ton of support and raised over $13,000. Maybe I just needed to find the right thing to raise funds for. Ten percent of the proceeds from this book will go toward breast cancer research and outreach.

Let's face it. We're aware of breast cancer. There are a ton of walks nationwide and pink products are everywhere. However, there are women who are still scared to get mammograms or go to the doctor after they discover something suspicious with their breasts. I wanted to help remove some of the fear that exists around breast health because early detection is so important.

Prior to writing this book, I read several breast cancer memoirs and the common thread in them was they covered diagnosis and treatment and that was the end of the story. They always left me wondering what happened next. Did they live beyond five years? Did they have a recurrence? What was their new "normal" like? So I decided I'd write a book that spanned from diagnosis to reaching the coveted five year cancer-free/survivorship anniversary. Thankfully, I made it.

Most of the names in the book have been changed to "protect the innocent" as they say. You'll notice sections called "Karla's Column" peppered throughout. That's what my husband at the time not so affectionately called the numerous emails and photos that I sent while I was battling cancer. He always felt like I was saying "Extra! Extra! Read all about it!" which worked his nerves. What can I say? I'm an open book. Through my candor I hope that you'll become more educated about breast cancer than you were before you started reading it. My goal was to tell a story that everyone, not just breast cancer survivors or people battling breast cancer, could identify with. That way I can save more breasts. Please read the book from cover to cover. There's information on breast health at the end.

Happy reading!

Survivorship: Year One

CHAPTER ONE:
A New Development

> *"Life is what happens to you while you're busy making other plans."*
>
> –John Lennon

From the moment I developed breasts I didn't like them. I got what I asked for so you would think I would've been happy. My mother, the daughter of a Baptist pastor, kept my three sisters and me in church enough that I knew I could ask God for anything and He would hear me. So I asked for breasts. I remember praying for breasts every night before bed. A girl at school was getting all the attention from the boys because she was starting to get what my older sisters called "mosquito bites"—not full on breasts but enough to need a training bra. I wanted the boys to notice me too. I know it sounds unbelievable but I woke up one morning and, *voila*, I had breasts. Real breasts! Not mosquito bites. The only problem was I had these marks on them. I rushed to show my mother my new breasts and the marks hoping she'd know how to get rid of them. The marks that is. She didn't know what they were but, being that she was a pharmaceutical sales representative, she knew a lot of doctors. If she didn't personally know a doctor I could see, she knew who to call to get a referral. I went to see a dermatologist who said the marks were stretch marks. I'd be stuck with them forever. They wouldn't go away but might fade with time. He explained that they come when your body grows faster than your skin's elasticity is ready for—for example, when you develop breasts overnight. I learned to be careful what I ask for.

That was the beginning of my antipathy toward my breasts and it wouldn't end anytime soon. A few years following my new development I was roughhousing with my sister and she punched me in my left breast. After that it never grew at the same pace as the right one. It could be a coincidence but I think she stunted the growth. So now I've got lopsided breasts with stretch marks, which I probably could have handled with the right bra and cover up makeup. It was when, for some reason, my full C atrophied to a small C which caused my breasts to sag that I thought I had the ugliest breasts on earth. Not sexy at all. I thought I'd never let a man see me topless but I got over it and learned that men don't pay as much attention to those kinds of things as women think they do. Besides, being a "sista," most men I dated weren't breasts men. They were booty men and thank God I had a booty that could make up for what I was lacking up top. I joke that my breasts were God's way of making sure I didn't become a pole dancer. I'm sure if I had beautiful breasts I'd have shown them off every chance I got.

As I got into my mid-to-late twenties I started to feel that my breasts weren't all *that* bad. They were very sensitive and could help me get to *that place* during sex, if you know what I mean. I didn't love my breasts but aside from the stretch marks they weren't anything a good plastic surgeon couldn't fix if I had the guts but I didn't. I always feared, because I was being too vain, that I'd have a botched surgery, like the ones I'd seen on TV. So I dealt with my breasts. I discovered if I pushed them up really good you could hardly tell I had stretch marks.

Some women have very strong feelings about their breasts. For me, they were just breasts. Not my best asset and certainly not the center of my world until one beautiful day in late August of 2007. I had recently relocated to the San Francisco Bay Area from my hometown of Seattle, WA having earned my MBA in Paris, France a year earlier. I had finally found a job after exactly a year of searching. There I was in my apartment doing what most people do who have recently relocated to a city where they don't know anyone—watching TV and being bored. Out of nowhere I felt a little itch on my left breast. I went into the bathroom to see what it was and noticed a slight rash. So I thought I would put a little cortisone cream on it and it would clear up in no time. As I was applying the cortisone cream I felt a large lump underneath the rash. I began to squeeze my breast to really get a feel for what was in there. The lump was quite large but I wasn't alarmed. I had had a clinical breast exam a month before coming to the Bay Area and I felt better than I had in years. I was losing a little weight from working out, going to yoga classes, and eating less junk. *Maybe my change in diet had caused a cyst*, I thought. Strange! In all of my thirty four years I'd never had a cyst in my breast but our bodies do behave differently as we get older.

Just as I'd done when I first developed breasts, I consulted my mother. When she picked up the phone, we chatted for a few minutes. I didn't want to startle her by jumping right into it. After I thought enough time had passed, I said, "So I'm calling because I found a lump in my breast."

"A what?" she said.

"A lump. I found a lump in my breast," I repeated.

"Ohhhh," she said with worry in her voice. "Well, have you changed your diet? Maybe you're drinking too much coffee." She was recalling a time in my tweens when I went to the doctor for shooting pains in my breasts and the doctor told me to lay off of caffeine. I loved colas and chocolate bars at the time and overdid it in those days. The doctor was right. When I cut back on my caffeine intake the pains went away. But at this time I was drinking mostly decaf which isn't caffeine free but has quite a bit less caffeine than regular coffee.

"Mom, I drank coffee just about every day when I was in Paris so why would I get a cyst from drinking it now?"

"Are you on your period? Maybe it came on because of your period."

"I am on my period. Hmmm."

"I don't know but Pat [one of her friends] has problems with her breasts like that. She gets cysts all the time. It's probably a cyst, baby, but you should have it checked out," she said with that voice of concern.

I told her I'd get a mammogram by any means necessary. I wouldn't let the doctor tell me that I'm too young for breast cancer or tell me to keep an eye on the lump and come back. I'd seen enough Oprah shows where women who had gone misdiagnosed of serious illnesses advised viewers to make sure doctors run all the right tests and not take no for an answer when they tell you it's in your head or you don't fit the demographic. I thought it would be strange and unlikely that I did have cancer but I was somewhat concerned. If I did have it I didn't want it to go undiagnosed. Time was of the essence.

I'd been saying that I'd go to the doctor for months. I'm asthmatic and was using my emergency inhaler as my daily maintenance, which is very dangerous. Finding this lump just put the fire under my butt. I had only been in Dublin, CA for four months when all of this happened. I didn't even have a doctor but I knew a friend at work, Diane, would know of a good one. She was one of those together women who always knew where to send you for lunch, a tailor, or a pedicure. She referred me to her primary care physician, Dr. Ferman, and his office was able to get me in within a week, which was pretty good for a new patient appointment.

When Dr. Ferman came in to the exam room he introduced himself and asked me what had brought me in. I started going on about my asthma because as time had passed and my period came closer to an end the lump started to shrink a little. Everyone told me that it must not be cancer because cancer doesn't shrink which made a lot of sense to me so I'd started to put the lump in the back of my mind. If Dr. Ferman hadn't brought it up I probably would have forgotten to mention it.

"What's this about a lump in your breast?" he said.

"Oh yeah! I found a lump in my left breast. I had a rash pop up and when I applied some cortisone cream to it I felt the lump underneath."

"Well, why don't you lie back and I'll do an exam?" he said.

I lay back and Dr. Ferman proceeded to do the typical breast exam where you walk your fingers across the breast covering every inch. The lump was hard to detect. I'd wondered how I could have missed it myself but becoming more familiar with it over the passing days I realized that it felt more like breast tissue or muscle when I rolled my fingers over it. I didn't think Dr. Ferman would find it with me lying down. Nevertheless, I lay back on the table. Maybe his medically trained hands would feel something that I hadn't.

"I don't feel anything," he said.

There went that theory. I sat up and said, "You can't find it like that. If I sit up and squeeze it, you can feel it." I grabbed the lump between my thumb and middle finger and he could clearly see the mass that was there.

He felt the lump and then felt under my arm and said, "Let's get you in for a mammogram and ultrasound. It's probably nothing but just to be safe." "How old are you?" he said, while looking through my chart.

"Thirty four." I replied

"Hmmm. Well, we'll have the mammogram and ultrasound and see what's going on in there." He had some concern in his voice but nothing that made me nervous. It was more like empathy—the kind of bedside manner that they're teaching these days in medical schools or doctors' conferences. It seemed to come from him naturally. I'd expected that I'd have to put up a fight with a new doctor to get a mammogram since I was too young for breast cancer in most people's minds, but that wasn't the case at all, which was a relief.

The doctor's office gave me the name of a place to schedule a mammogram. It was early September but they didn't have any available appointments until mid-October. I wanted to get in sooner but if the imaging center didn't think it was urgent maybe it wasn't. I'm sure all of their patients thought their mammograms were life or death as well so I didn't want to be pushy. About a week went by and my dad called to see when my mammogram was scheduled. I told him sometime in October. He said, "You shouldn't wait that long. You need to call someplace else and see if they can get you in sooner, baby. It's not anything to play around with. Remember your grandmother had breast cancer."

His mother, Grandma Laurel, died of breast cancer in 2004. She must have had it for years before anyone discovered it because the tumor had broken through her skin. My dad's side of the family is West Indian and I think my grandma thought she had some sort of island cure for it. Supposedly, her mother had had "issues" with her breasts and put some sort of salve on them and healed herself so my grandmother thought she could do the same. She was staying with my uncle and aunt at the time. It wasn't until my aunt started to get curious about how much gauze and wound dressings my grandmother was having her buy that they realized my grandmother was treating open wounds on her breasts. She was eighty-two when she was diagnosed and she lived just as full a life as anyone until her death a couple of years later. After her diagnosis she had cataracts surgery and was very excited to be able to read her Bible without glasses. She was taking piano lessons and was the life of the center where she was being treated.

I'd always marveled at my grandmother. I remembered in 1997, the last time she'd come to Seattle to visit she'd been in her seventies then and wore three and a half inch heels. She'd told us that she stayed fit because she ate Cream of Wheat with wheat germ daily and did floor exercises every morning including full push-ups—several of them, which she showed us just in case we thought she was a lightweight. We'd laugh when she'd tell us that she could never move to Seattle no matter how hard we tried to persuade her. It was too boring she said. She loved New York and couldn't imagine living anywhere else. She was full of life. She and my maternal grandmother were like night and day. Grandma Reed, who was the quintessential black church's pastor's wife, was more of a virtuous woman and a lot more strict. Grandma Reed could cook like nobody's business, was a milliner and a furrier who made fierce hats and coats. She was just an all-around stylish woman but she didn't play around. You didn't want to piss her off or you might have to go outside and pick out a switch for her to use on your back-side. I never tested her.

Both of my grandmothers were amazing women but my paternal grandmother was the fun grandma. I'm sure my dad was concerned that I might be like her and wait so long to be treated that my chances of survival would be lessened. My grandma lived to be eighty-four, which is quite an accomplishment. However, if she'd sought treatment sooner I believe she would be alive today.

Maybe the call from my dad was the push that I needed. I called the image center again and to my surprise they had an appointment that week. No one said anything to me about being booked until October. It was like I called an entirely different place. My father was relieved because I'd told him that I'd started to notice some changes in my breast. My nipple and underarm had started to swell and I started to feel like something was living in my breast. I know people say that cancer doesn't hurt and you can't feel cancer but I beg to differ and one of my survivor friends agrees with me. I'd feel shooting pains in my breast every now and then. I also felt like some sort of chemical reaction was going on in my breast. It was like in a sci-fi movie when the alien invaded someone's body and you could see it moving under the person's skin. In my case I couldn't see it but I sure could feel it. Something foreign was inside of me and I knew that it needed to come out. Not to mention that I'd done what most people tell you not to do if you have a cancer scare. I'd gone online and done research. That was my modus operandi. It started when I'd discovered my mother's Merck Manual as a young girl. The Merck Manual contained just about every disease imaginable to man. If I had an ailment I looked it up and I'd know what it was and what it wasn't so I could communicate that to the doctor. I wasn't about to be misdiagnosed. Nowadays, all you need is the Internet and I'd seen and read all kinds of things that said my symptoms pointed to cancer. I was anxious to have the mammogram and ultrasound done so that I could get to the bottom of what was happening.

CHAPTER TWO:
What's Old is New Again

"Life always offers you a second chance. It's called tomorrow"

–Unknown

After returning from Paris, the Bay Area was the last place I thought I'd be. I was willing and excited to relocate anywhere in the world but purposely didn't apply for jobs in California. My ex-husband, Jamal, was in the Bay Area the last I'd heard and I just didn't think there was room enough for the two of us. When I finally found a job as a Client Solutions Manager for a market research company and they told me that I would be moving to Northern California, I knew it was a possibility that I could run into him. I went back and forth about writing a letter (care of his mom since I didn't have his address) to let him know that I was in the area. It had been four or five years since I'd spoken with him but he'd been my husband at one point. I couldn't imagine bumping into him at Wal-Mart or something and making small talk like we were former classmates. I just didn't know what Jamal I would be reaching out to. Jamal was a handsome, former college football player that had put on some extra pounds. He was a big guy, (about 6'2" and 255 pounds when I saw him last), who if you didn't know him and he wasn't smiling you could probably be intimidated by him. Despite his hard looking exterior he was very charming and was always the life of the party. He liked to call himself a chameleon because he could fit in and have a good time anywhere and with anyone.

Jamal was very attractive but I was wondering if he still had some of the qualities that I didn't find so attractive. When we were married he liked to drink, which I'd known when I met him but soon after we married he took a liking to gambling and basically told me that he wasn't going to give up either so if that's what I wanted I'd better move on. He didn't have to tell me twice. It was unfortunate because I liked to drink and gamble too. I just knew when to stop. He didn't.

The last time I'd spoken to Jamal he'd really hurt me by saying that I hadn't done anything with my life since we'd divorced (not that he was doing anything with his) and that it was my fault that our marriage hadn't worked. I told him that most people I knew thought very highly of me and he was the only one who didn't. He was the only person in my life who'd ever put me down and I was tired of it so I cut him off. We didn't have any ties to each other. He has a son, Jamal Jr. or J.J. but we didn't have any kids together. We had tried but our four pregnancies ended in miscarriages. With nothing connecting us, the years just went by with no communication. I thought about him from time to time, just hoping that he was okay but never with the idea of rekindling our relationship. When I divorced him, God spoke to my spirit and let me know that I would remarry him which I didn't understand at the time. In my mind he could never be the kind of man that I wanted in my life. But I knew if it was God I wouldn't need to do anything. It would just happen. I did find it strange that I wound up in the Bay Area of all places though.

After much contemplation, I decided to go ahead and send a letter. In hindsight, I think the cancer scare had an influence on my decision.

Karla's Column

September 5, 2007

Hi Jamal:

I'm sure you can tell who this is by the name at the top of the letter. It's been quite a long time since I've spoken with you and I hope and trust that things are going well for you. I relocated to the Bay Area in May and wondered how you were doing. The last time I spoke with you I think you were living in Hayward, which is pretty close to Dublin where I live. I just wanted you to know that I'm here. I thought it would be pretty awkward to run into you somewhere since this is probably the last place you'd expect to see me. It's the last place I would've expected to be too but after graduate school this is where opportunity presented itself. Surprisingly, I'm actually enjoying the Bay Area. I can't think of anywhere else in the U.S. that I'd rather be.

So that's what's going on in my life. My family is alive and well. They ask about you from
time to time. How's your family? I think
about J.J. all the time and wonder how tall
he is and how he's progressing.

Well I won't write a long letter. I just wanted
to say hello and see how you're doing. The
last time that I spoke with you, you didn't
have too many nice things to say to me.
Maybe enough time has passed that we can
be friends. My contact information is below.
Drop me a line or give me a call.

Take care,

Karla

The weekend before my mammogram Jamal called me. His
mother had forwarded him my letter. He said that he was on
his way to Stockton (about a forty five minute drive from me),
which is where he and his family are from. It was his birthday
weekend and he had a job interview lined up for the following
Monday. He was living in Las Vegas but had been exploring
career opportunities in California. We talked briefly about how
our families and J.J. were doing and then decided to meet for
lunch since he was in town.

Seeing that Jamal had driven all the way from Las Vegas and
I wanted to see his family, I met him at his parents' house. It was
nice to see his parents. They were happy to see me. To my surprise
it was actually really nice to see Jamal too. He'd put on quite a bit

of weight. I thought he looked like a big teddy bear. I could tell he was still the same fun, charming guy that I had loved. I was wondering if he was still drinking and gambling. He was living in Las Vegas where there is no shortage of liquor *or* casinos.

We went to a Mexican restaurant for lunch and sat by the window which had a view of a manmade lake. Jamal took over the conversation as if he had a lot to say and had finally gotten the opportunity to say it.

"Karla, I've been trying to find you. I'd see women in Las Vegas who looked like you, run up to them, and tap them on the shoulder. I'd have to say 'Sorry. I thought you were someone else.' I talked about you so much to my friends that they were starting to think that I was making you up." He said with excitement in his voice. I smiled. It was nice to know that he missed me and realized he messed up a good thing.

Then he said to me what I thought I'd never hear from him; "I take full responsibility for our marriage not working." That's when I knew he'd changed. The old Jamal would never have admitted that he was wrong.

"I want a second chance to prove to you that I'm different." He confessed.

"Are you still drinking and gambling? You live in Vegas. That's not the best place to be if you like to drink and gamble too much." I said.

He said living in Vegas had taken the appeal out of drinking and gambling. He said he didn't have a problem with either anymore. Jamal and I always had a great connection and we always had a lot of fun together. If I could have my husband back without the issues we had previously, I thought that would be great. It had been a little over five years since we divorced and I hadn't even so much as seen let alone met anyone that interested me.

After he poured his heart out I thought it was a good time to let him know that I could be facing a serious battle. One that he would have to face with me should we remarry. "I found a lump in my breast. I have a mammogram next week. I'm hoping it's nothing" I said. He reached for my hand and said "I want to be there for you. Even if I'm not physically here I want you to call my family. You know they love you and still consider you family." I could tell that he was concerned about the cancer and me not having my family near but he mostly wanted the opportunity to show that he would be supportive.

To my surprise I didn't want the afternoon to end so I invited him to stay the night. We made love (we always did move pretty quickly) and in the morning I made him a hearty omelet for breakfast. He always loved for me to make him omelets on weekend mornings when we were married.

My family was happy to hear that Jamal had changed and we were considering getting back together. They always loved him in spite of our issues and they were glad that if I did have to battle cancer I wouldn't be alone.

Jamal and I knew that we would need time to start anew. We had a lot to overcome—baggage from our marriage, distance. He was living in Las Vegas and I was living in the Bay Area. It was possible that he could have a job offer in Stockton but it wasn't a definite. He was planning to stay for about a week and then he'd make a decision about this job if it was offered to him. Our reunion would be challenging but we'd just take things one day at a time.

CHAPTER THREE:
On the Verge

"Life's too short to sweat the small stuff."

–Unknown

I kept getting those looks like "what are you doing here?" as I sat in the waiting area of the image center. I was clearly the youngest patient there. They finally called me back after keeping me waiting for what seemed like a lifetime. They did the mammogram first and the experience wasn't as bad as I thought it would be. I was expecting it to be painful or very uncomfortable, having your breasts placed in the machine and flattened, but my pendulous breasts were no problem. There are some plusses to having saggy breasts.

While I waited for the mammography film to develop a technician took me into a different room to perform the ultrasound. She glided the wand over my lubricated breast and underarm to get a look at my lymph nodes. As she pressed the wand deeply into the pit of my arm, I could tell that she saw something of interest. She'd been pretty chatty up until that point. Then all of a sudden she got quiet. I knew something wasn't right. She kept sliding the wand over my armpit while simultaneously hitting the keys on the keyboard to capture the image. When she finished she told me the radiologist would be in shortly to go over the images.

The radiologist came in, lubricated me again, and gave me the once over with the wand herself. The technician told her that she thought she'd seen something under my arm but the radiologist didn't seem to see anything when she looked. She was rather delicate with her touch so I told her that the technician had pressed harder. She told me that it didn't matter how hard one pressed. If there was something there it would show up. I didn't believe her so I kept a mental note of the possibility, in case I did wind up having lymph node trouble.

She gave me a towel to wipe off my breast and said she'd be right back. When she returned, she looked at me and said, "I want to be honest with you. There is a tumor in your breast and it looks aggressive. I'm going to call your PCP [primary care physician] right now and he'll want to refer you to a breast surgeon right away." She didn't say anything about a biopsy. She seemed pretty sure that we needed to remove it ASAP. I think she was surprised, maybe even disappointed, that I didn't cry but I was already prepared for the news since I had done some research of my own. She was just confirming what I already suspected. Not to mention, I had been at my emotional lowest eight years prior when I was going through my divorce, suffering from hypothyroidism, dealing with the miscarriages and depression all which took their toll on me and caused me to burnout at work. I wasn't about to go there again. I thanked her and started getting dressed.

Something about leaving the dark, quiet ultrasound room and walking out of the building into the bustling business area on that beautiful, sunny day was symbolic of what I was about to face. I was going to be in a dark, solitary place but life would not miss a beat. While I was getting the bad news and my world seemed to come to a halt, cars were still driving down the street, leaves blowing in the wind, people walking to and fro just as they were before I had my mammogram. My life was about to change forever and, although everyone would be there for support, no one could get inside my head and experience my emotions or feel my pain. I would be going somewhere that only I could go.

It was while walking from the image center to my car that I instinctively dug in my heels. Like being outside during a windstorm and bracing yourself for the next gust of wind. You have to bear down and choose a stance that will prevent the storm from getting the best of you. I refused to be moved. Now was not the time to shrink. It was time to stand tall.

Without making a conscious effort I set the tone for how I and my family would approach my battle. On the way to my car I called my parents to tell them what the radiologist had said. I wasn't hysterical or bawling or sounding doomed. I had to be strong so that everyone else would be strong. My dad answered and I told him that they thought it was cancer. He said, "Oh boy. What are they going to do?"

"The radiologist said that she is going to call Dr. Ferman right away and get me scheduled for surgery."

"Are they sure?" he said.

"She thinks so but I need to hear from Dr. Ferman to find out what to do next."

I spoke to Dr. Ferman that afternoon and he said that he was going to refer me to his wife's breast surgeon. I found out later that his wife had been diagnosed with breast cancer the year before, which might explain the empathy he had for me. I took solace in knowing that my doctor was referring me to doctors to whom he entrusted his own wife. He told me that he didn't want me to have surgery just yet but he did want me to have a biopsy. That way we would know for sure if it was breast cancer and find out what stage it was.

I called the breast surgeon and the receptionist was very nice. She didn't have any appointments available but pulled some strings and got me scheduled for Tuesday of the next week at six thirty in the morning before their first patient. On one hand I was very happy that I wasn't being pushed off. On the other hand their accommodation made me feel like they knew my situation was dire.

Through all of this I was living alone in a city that I'd only been in for four months. I had some friends but hadn't formed any close bonds with anyone. On top of that, I was frustrated with my new job. The onboarding left a lot to be desired. I was based out of my client's office and was basically thrown into the position with no training and faced with questions day in and day out that I was expected to know the answers to but didn't.

It had taken me exactly a year to find a job after earning my MBA, which was way longer than I'd anticipated. I thought I'd be so marketable with my language skills and international experience having studied in Paris, but was discouraged by the reality that there weren't a lot of jobs that interested me and it seemed there were more MBAs looking for jobs than there were jobs. There were also a lot of jobs that required an MBA from a top tier school, which mine was not.

When I realized my job hunt wasn't going according to plan, I resorted to doing temporary work and living off of my credit cards. So when I got the offer it was just in the nick of time because I was so broke I couldn't pay attention. I contemplated not taking the position because they told me that I needed to pay for my relocation and they would reimburse me. I didn't have the money to relocate myself but it wasn't like I had offers piling up. I reasoned with myself that the job paid pretty well, offered skills that I wanted to acquire, and I'd have one of the largest consumer packaged goods companies, PepsiCo, as my client, so I accepted.

I wound up borrowing the money from my dad for the move. I rented a U-Haul, leased an apartment online, sight unseen, and arranged for a rental car until I had enough money to buy a car, since I had given up my dream car in a Lemon Law mediation and used the money to live on in Paris. I would get $5,000 as a relocation bonus but wouldn't receive it until I was on the payroll for two weeks. The recruiter promised me that she would "babysit" the reimbursement process so that I'd get my check right away but somehow it slipped through the cracks.

Two months into the job, I still hadn't received my reimbursement check but my company finally saw fit to send me to Chicago for training. They booked me in a nice, historic hotel in a prestigious part of Chicago called Gold Coast. Everything was lovely. The bellmen were friendly and accommodating, the lobby had beautiful floral arrangements with my favorite flowers (stargazer lilies and roses) and I had a nice size room with a king size bed. Maybe my company isn't that bad, I thought.

Almost immediately after I got settled into my room, my colleague and fellow new hire, Hena, who was based out of New York and also had her share of grievances with the company, called me and said, "Did you know we're paying for our rooms?" I said, "No we're not. They asked me for my card for incidentals but they didn't say anything about paying for the room." She told me that she was sure that we had to pay for the rooms ourselves.

That night, Hena and I went out to dinner with our boss,

who was also a recent hire, his boss, and the other trainees. My boss's boss, Elaine, who was sitting one person away from me decided to make small talk.

"How do you guys like the hotel?"

I said, "It's nice. I like it a lot." Then I said to her in a low voice, my lips kind of closed, "Are we paying for the room?"

Hena was looking at me just waiting to get the scoop. Elaine looked at me like she was surprised that I was surprised and nonchalantly said, "Uhn hun, just put it on a card and expense it."

What?! How did she think I'd been surviving as a recent graduate who relocated to one of the most expensive areas of the U.S. on my own dime?

"I don't have a card. My cards are maxed with all I've had to do over the last two months."

She knew full well what was going on with my relocation bonus. I'd sent an email to payroll earlier that day that she was CC'd on in which I explained that two months after being hired I still hadn't received my relocation bonus. I let them know that I was planning to pick up my check in person since I was in Chicago. I was basically telling them that I wasn't leaving town without my reimbursement check.

I guess the look on my face let Elaine know that she needed to do some damage control so she remarked, "By the way, that other situation is taken care of," implying that I'd get my reimbursement as if that was some sort of consolation for unexpectedly having to pay for my hotel room (a little over $400). I hate surprises of the negative kind and this company had given me too many. Once again, daddy to the rescue. My company was starting to wear him out too.

Those are some of the stressors that I was dealing with leading up to finding the lump and then something happened to put me over the edge. One of my lifelong friends from Seattle, Tina, and some of her girlfriends were coming to Sacramento. Tina's friend, Monica has a sister and brother in law who were part owners of a restaurant and they were having their grand opening. Tina and her girlfriends know how to party so I knew I'd be in for a good time. I drove two hours to Sacramento and was planning not to party too hard so that I could drive back that night.

The restaurant was located in an upscale outdoor mall which must have been the hot spot because there were tons of fabulous people everywhere. There was no available self-parking for blocks so luckily, the restaurant had complimentary valet parking. I had great food and drinks and we danced all night to live music. Once the grand opening crowd died down we bar hopped and then found our way back to the restaurant and danced some more. The thought of getting my keys from the valet crossed my mind but since I was at the restaurant with the owners I figured the valet wouldn't close down without letting the restaurant know that they hadn't returned all of the keys. I was having such a good time that I decided to stay the night with the girls in their hotel room, which was practically connected to the restaurant. When we finally called it a night, I asked the owners about my keys and they said they were probably in the restaurant somewhere and we could look in the morning. If they didn't find them we could call the valet company. Sounded simple enough.

The next morning my keys (car and apartment keys on the same key ring) were nowhere to be found. My car was parked in front of the restaurant but we had no idea where the keys were. We called the valet company and they said it wasn't their policy to close down without returning all keys to their customers. They were trying to get hold of the people that had worked the valet the previous night, to no avail. Tina and her girlfriends had a flight to catch back to Seattle and the restaurant owners had other obligations too. I was stranded in Sacramento waiting for the valet company to let me know how they were going to resolve the situation. Several hours later, when it seemed like there was nothing else I could do, I decided to catch a cab to a car rental place and rent a car so that I could drive to Dublin and get my spare keys. My apartment leasing office would close before I would make it there. I needed someone to go to my apartment leasing office and get my spare apartment key so that I could get my spare car key. I had met a guy who lived in the Bay Area on my first (and last) foray into online dating. There wasn't a love connection but I considered him a friend and knew I could lean on him in time of need. Bless his heart, he drove to my apartment, got the key and had it waiting for me when I arrived. Then he followed me back to the car rental office in Sacramento to drop off my rental and drove me back to the restaurant. When we pulled up in his truck the headlights shined on my rear, passenger tire and I saw something glistening. It was my car keys! They'd been sitting in the wheel well the whole day. I was so frustrated that the valet company couldn't have told me to look there. What if someone else had noticed the keys before I had? My car could have been stolen. I was so pissed! I spent the better part of the next week trying to get the valet company to reimburse me for my expenses.

That experience just reiterated the importance of family and close friends, of which I had neither in the area. This relocation to the Bay Area had turned out to be worse than relocating to France, where I'd only had an elementary command of the language when I arrived.

The following day was Monday and on the way to work I called my mom to vent. I was frustrated because I was tight for money since I'd had the unexpected valet fiasco. I was telling her how none of it would have happened if I had family or close friends there. I could have just called someone with a spare car key like my parents or sisters instead of having to inconvenience someone I'd only known for such a short time. I'd barely gotten any sleep the night before due to all of the trips I'd had to make to Sacramento. All of a sudden mid rant the tears started flowing and I said, "And what if I have cancer. I'll be here all by myself!" I surprised myself. I'm not usually so emotional but I reached my breaking point. I think the combination of the job, the valet situation, my finances, having a lump in my breast that was probably cancerous, and feeling alone (not lonely but alone) sent me over the edge.

"Don't cry baby. You know if you have cancer momma will be on the next plane flying to see about her baby."

"I know mom. I think I'm just upset about the money that I had to spend over this stupid valet thing and how they treated me. Everything is such a struggle."

"When is your appointment for the biopsy?"

"Tomorrow at six thirty a.m."

"I'm going to see if I can get a ticket so that I can go with you." And my mom came to town that very night.

CHAPTER FOUR:
Dessert before Dinner

"Life is short. Eat dessert first."

– Unknown

$\mathcal{M}$y breast surgeon, Dr. Kendrick, had a very nicely decorated office with a lot of Willow Tree Angels scattered around. They are the cute little blank faced angels with wire for the wings. At the time I didn't know who made the figurines but I loved them. They were so inspiring and beautiful. When Dr. Kendrick entered the exam room, she introduced herself and put my mammogram on the X-Ray view box. She explained that my tumor looked suspicious. She didn't say anything about whether or not she thought I had cancer but she explained to me what would happen if I did. She told me that she was going to do a core biopsy where she would make a small incision around my areola and insert a tool that would take a small portion of my tumor. She would then send it to pathology and have the results in two days.

She took me in a neighboring exam room to do the biopsy

while my mother waited in the other exam room. She said it would be less distracting for me if no one was in the room. She also didn't want anyone else's reaction to make me lose my cool. I stared at the ceiling while she numbed my areola and made the incision. Then she inserted the core biopsy tool which looked like a long, skinny apple corer, pulled the trigger and it took a cylindrical piece out of the tumor. I didn't really feel a thing.

Just before she finished up the biopsy she told me that she wasn't going to patronize me because she could see that I was an intelligent young woman. She confessed that my tumor looked cancerous and she proceeded to give me a folder with breast cancer resources and information on the hospital where she performed surgery. I was glad that she didn't keep me in the dark. Once again we were pretty sure it was cancer but still didn't know for certain. I made an appointment to come back two days later to get the results.

That Thursday my mother and I went back to Dr. Kendrick's office and she broke the news to me. I had Stage II Invasive Ductal Carcinoma. I'd caught it early which I was happy about. I wouldn't be a part of the statistic that says black women usually find their breast cancer at stage III or later. I'm not sure what spurs that statistic—lack of health care coverage, less breast self-exams, etc.—but I felt relieved that I was on top of it. I'd most likely need to have surgery and radiation. But I was going to try to avoid chemotherapy at all costs. I didn't want to put my body through that. It's actually the chemo that makes you look like death warmed over, not the cancer. I looked and felt just fine and I wanted to keep it that way. I wasn't at all concerned about losing my hair. I just didn't want to be made sick and depressed.

I also had the choice of having a lumpectomy or a mastectomy. I chose the latter. I decided that my breasts were saggy enough so I didn't want to remove any breast tissue without replacing the volume. I thought this could be my chance to get a breast lift. California law stipulates that reconstructive surgery on one breast has to include augmentation of the unaffected breast, if necessary, to create symmetry. My mother thought it strange that I'd want to have my breast removed but I had never liked my breasts anyway so I saw it as an opportunity to get the breasts I'd always wanted. Maybe go braless sometimes. Not to mention, I was only thirty-four and the chances of recurrence in my lifetime were higher since I was so young. Another reason I opted for a mastectomy is that I just felt like my breast cancer was a little more serious than the doctors thought. My underarm had started to swell and I thought the cancer had spread to my lymph nodes. Dr. Kendrick examined my underarm and thought it was just irritated. Yeah! I thought. Irritated by cancer! What else would irritate it?

I'd have surgery in the following three to four weeks. My cancer didn't appear to be fast growing so we had time.

My mom and I broke the news to my dad and sisters and I told Jamal. Everyone took it really well since leading up to the biopsy everything was pointing in the direction of cancer. They also knew that I was wanting and needing them to be strong.

That evening, my mom, Jamal, and I went out to dinner. As soon as we were seated my mother and I both reached for the dessert menu. The day's news called for dessert before dinner. I don't recall us ever doing that before but somehow we read each other's minds. We both instinctively knew that a pick-me-up was in order. Jamal was surprised by our being so in sync. He'd never heard of such a thing and thought it must have been something that we did routinely. My mother and I said to him at the same time, "Life is short, that's why you should eat dessert first." It made perfect sense to us, especially on that day.

<u>Karla's Column</u>

In this email to my family and friends I told my story in great detail because I wanted them to know what to do if this happened to them and to know the warning signs of breast cancer.

Good News and Bad News

From: Karla (karla@email.com)

Sent: 9/30/2007 2:19 PM

To: Family & Friends

Hello Everyone,

I have some good news and some bad news. Unfortunately, it's pretty personal news that I'd prefer to tell everyone over the phone but it's more convenient to say it once via email. I was diagnosed with breast cancer last Thursday. About a month ago I had a rash on my breast and when I felt it I felt a cyst underneath. The cyst was actually rather large so I wasn't too alarmed because I figured I'd been doing my breast self-exams and had had a clinical breast exam in April before I left Seattle. I figured if it were cancer it wouldn't grow that fast all of a sudden. It started to go down so everyone thought it must be a cyst because cancer wouldn't shrink, it would grow. I do get my share of caffeine, which is a cyst catalyst, although I drank more coffee when I lived in Paris so I wasn't really sold on the cyst idea. I decided to go to the doctor and ask for a mammogram anyway. It was my first visit to this doctor since I've only been here five months. I went in knowing that even though I'm thirty four and not due for a mammogram until forty I'd insist that my doctor refer me to a clinic. He didn't hesitate to send me just to put my mind at ease. After I saw him I noticed that my underarm was more swollen than the right underarm and my areola had started to puff up. I couldn't get in for a mammogram until October 10th but my parents pushed me to find another place that could take me. I called a clinic that I'd called previously and they got me in that following Monday (last Monday). I'd been doing my research and knew that what I was experiencing (even though the lump had shrunk) didn't sound good. The radiologist confirmed my suspicions but my doctor wanted me to have a biopsy to be sure. My mom flew in to be there for my biopsy the next day. The biopsy came back Thursday and what I have is Infiltrating (Invasive) Ductal Carcinoma-Stage II http://www.cancer.org/docroot/CRI/content/CRI_2_2_1X_What_is_breast_cancer_5.asp?sitearea=. It doesn't appear to be in my lymph nodes, which is good but we won't be certain until I have surgery in the next few weeks and they can examine my lymph nodes. If it's not in my lymph nodes then I won't have to do chemo. They would suggest radiation unless I have a mastectomy, which would remove everything so there wouldn't be a risk of it spreading or returning. I'm leaning toward the mastectomy because I'm in my thirties and I have several years ahead of me in which time it's likely that it would return. Also I would have my breast reconstructed which sounds appealing to me. If I have to go through this I might as well come out looking better than before. Not to mention, if they do the lumpectomy they aren't sure how much of my breast they would have to take so who knows what it would look like afterwards. So it's pretty hard to believe that I have breast cancer. I'm so grateful that I knew the symptoms of inflammatory breast cancer which I don't have but some of my symptoms (the rash, under arm swelling, and areola changes) were similar so it made me take notice and take them seriously. Even when I went in to the doctor he couldn't feel the lump when I lay down on the table. I'd never felt it lying down or standing to do my breast exam as they suggest. When I squeezed I felt it because it's hard and when you feel around like you're feeling for a pebble it felt like my muscle or normal tissue. I've heard that a lot of women say their husbands found their lump and I think it's because a husband would be squeezing his wife's breast not feeling around for a pebble sized lump. So my advice to all the ladies is to really examine your breasts. Anything that's unusual, even on the skin, research it so that when you tell your doctor they can rule things out that concern you. My surgeon said that I've probably had cancer for three to five years so it's spreading but it's a slow growing cancer. Over those three to five years I've had doctors examine my breast and no one including myself felt anything out of the ordinary. I thank God that I found it when I did.

So that's the bad news. The good news is that just a few days before the diagnosis I reconnected with my ex-husband and he's a changed man and so happy to have a second chance to be a husband to me (a picture of me and my teddy bear as I call him now is attached). Before I knew exactly what was wrong with me I called my mom crying and fed up with all of the obstacles I've had since I've been in Cali and I said 'What if something is wrong with me? I'll be here all by myself.' She assured me that she'd be there in a heartbeat and she was, which meant a lot to me but when she leaves at least I have someone who I know loves and cares for me to go through this with me. My in-laws are very excited to see me and Jamal get back together. So I'm not going through this alone and I know all of you will be praying for and thinking of me as well. Know that I'm still the same Karla I was before the diagnosis. Everyone is quite surprised that I'm going through anything. I haven't cried about it because I think I was prepared for it and there are good things happening along with the bad. That being said, if you reach out to me don't call crying and carrying on because it's not that type of party. Just pray and believe. The Lord healed me once and I know He can do it again.

Love you!

Karla

CHAPTER FIVE:
The Paris Years

"Paris is always a good idea."

–Audrey Hepburn

*A*fter returning to the States from Paris, I often wondered if it had been a good idea to live abroad. I'd racked up a lot of credit card debt, I had a huge student loan, and I wondered how long it would take me to get from under the mountain that I'd created. Receiving a cancer diagnosis makes you take inventory of your life. *Is this it? Did I have a good life if it should end soon? Did I live life to the fullest?*

Living in Paris was one of those dreams that kept gnawing at me. I talked about it ad nauseam to anyone who would listen. I'm sure, when I finally left, everyone was happy that they didn't have to hear about how much I longed to be in Paris anymore. All in all, I had the most memorable time of my life but sometimes, because of the debt I incurred, I wondered, was it worth it?

Bitten by the Paris Bug

My mother and I had always dreamed about going to Paris. She'd taken French in high school and college. So, wanting to be like her, I did the same. I'd sit at the kitchen table while she cooked and she'd help me study my French lessons. We told each other that one day we'd go to Paris together. Several years later, my mom had been bumped from a flight. She'd kept the voucher she received as consolation, tacked to her bulletin board in her home office. Several months after being bumped she was cleaning up her office and heard a still small voice say to her *"Call about Paris."* When she made the call to reservations, she found out that fares were really low. She wound up paying seven dollars for a round trip ticket. As soon as she booked her ticket, she called to tell me that she was going to Paris and I said, "Not without me you aren't." Her friend Patricia was of the same mind and Patricia's sister-in-law, Donna, wanted to come too. Ironically, the four of us were all at turning points in our lives. Patricia had just quit her job of twenty plus years to become a real estate agent—a bold move for a single woman who was used to a steady paycheck. Donna, whose first marriage was to Patricia's late brother, was in a bad second marriage and caring for her ailing parents. I was separated from Jamal and at a crossroads with my job, and my mom was always in the process of leaving my dad. Not to mention that her life was pretty monotonous and predictable. She worked, took care of her family, and played piano and sang at church. She was in desperate need of some excitement in her life.

We fell in love with Paris from the minute our shuttle hit *L'Avenue des Champs Élysées*—especially all of the beautiful architecture, the gold accents on the buildings and monuments. Everything was so opulent. I remember, when I saw *L'Arc de Triomphe* up close for the first time, something came over me. Before that, it was all about the Eiffel Tower or *La Tour Eiffel* for me. But when I saw *L'Arc de Triomphe* I was literally in awe. All I could do was stare at it but it wasn't one of those situations where I was staring because there was so much to take in. It was like I was being spoken to. From that experience I knew Paris had something in store for me and that I'd be back. Why and in what capacity I didn't know but I'd definitely be back.

Paris was a place where I felt like I fit in. It seemed that someone always tried to put you in a box in the States. A young, black woman couldn't appreciate art, classical music, or fine wine and food without being considered bougie or uppity. At that time in my life I was on the verge of walking away from my sales job with a Fortune 500 company because I was burnt out. The marriage, the miscarriages, my hypothyroidism, and drive to succeed in spite of everything that was going on in my life had taken its toll on me. When I was in France I saw a lifestyle that made more sense—a slower pace of life. Parisians took time to smell the roses. No one rushed you out of a restaurant. You could linger at a table and no one bugged you about ordering more food. It was a totally new experience for me, a new pace of life, and I loved it.

Everything about my first trip felt like destiny. It was like we were there to see the possibilities and instead of asking ourselves "why?" ask "why not?" or "Pourquoi pas?" It was the mantra of the trip. I told our waiter at a restaurant close to our hotel that I loved Paris so much that I wanted to move there. He said to me, "Pourquoi pas?" When we left the restaurant we saw a boutique called, *Pourquoi pas?* We seemed to keep hearing or seeing that phrase. Interestingly enough, in subsequent trips I never heard anyone say it and the *Pourquoi Pas?* Boutique was closed. I happened to take a picture of it since it was our mantra and I still have it to remind me to consider the possibilities in life.

During our week and a half stay, we saw all of the traditional sites but also did some non-conventional things. We learned about Ricki Stevenson, a U.S. expatriate and former news reporter/talk show host, who'd started a business in Paris called Black Paris Tours. She took us off the beaten path to see where Josephine Baker, Richard Wright, and other famous African Americans lived and hung out. We also heard of a gospel brunch and thought that would be a nice way to spend our last Sunday in Paris. The restaurant, Chesterfield Café, was an American style pub right off the *Champs Élysées*, which is the widest, most popular street in Paris. Midway through the performers' set Patricia excused herself to go to the restroom. On her way, she told the restaurant manager that my mom was a gospel singer from the U.S. and asked if she could sing a song. Before we'd left the States, we'd joked about my mom singing in Paris, but now we had our mantra for a little inspiration. My mom spent her life singing in church. She would have loved to have taken her singing outside of those four walls but her parents wouldn't hear of it. She was a pastor's child and needed to live like one. Now her father was thousands of miles away and her mother had gone on to glory so there was nothing to stand in her way. They called her up to the stage and asked her if she knew "This Little Light of Mine." We knew it was destiny because the Sunday before we left for our trip our pastor prayed for us and asked God to "let her light shine" through her gift of song. After he prayed we sang "This Little Light of Mine." Of all the gospel songs in the world the choir in Paris asked her to sing that one. She sang, "This little light of mine. I'm gonna let it shine. Everywhere I go. I'm gonna let it shine." The audience gave her a standing ovation. They loved her so much that the promoter asked for her CD (as if she were a professional) and said that he wanted to bring her back to Paris to do concerts. *"Pourquoi Pas?"* we said. By the end of that trip all four of us wanted to make our way back to Paris. We knew from this trip that we just needed to believe.

When we returned to the States, my mother quickly produced a CD and returned to Paris to sing. I was still working and wasn't able to make the trip. Not long after that, however, I left my job and since I was unemployed I became her manager. It didn't pay well but I welcomed any opportunity to visit Paris until I figured out when and how I could live there. I went back to Paris and Europe several times within a two year span accompanying her on her singing gigs mainly because she is epileptic and needed someone with her who was familiar with her condition.

I'd never really dreamed of working for someone else. I always wanted to be an entrepreneur. In fact, I put myself through manicuring school on one of my summer breaks from college. It was always my dream to own my own skincare and cosmetics line but at the time black women were more into nails than skincare. I planned to build my nail clientele and then convert them to skin clients. My last year of college I opened my nail shop inside my mother's consignment store, Edna's Second Chance, whose motto was "Give your clothes a second chance to make a first impression." I thought of that myself. Pretty clever! We called it Edna's Second Chance not only because of the nature of the business but because of the fact that my mom, Edna, had

had one failed business attempt before the consignment shop. I should have known not to go into business with her but I didn't listen to my inner wisdom. My mom has a lot of great ideas but she isn't the most savvy businesswoman. She closed up shop two months after I moved in. My investment in my salon and my dreams of being self-employed all went down the drain.

When I went to Paris the first time, being at a crossroads in my career, I thought about following my dream again. Paris is known for esthetics and would have been the perfect place to study skin. Everyone there that I told about my esthetics goals thought it was the most wonderful thing. That's the other thing that really attracted me to Paris. It seemed like they were more interested in a person's passion rather than how they were paying the bills. No one asked me the number one question that Americans love to ask and people without a job hate to hear. "What do you do?" Not one person I met in Paris asked me that.

The esthetician plans never panned out. I didn't have the money to make that a reality especially after leaving my job. I wasn't totally without income. I was supplementing what I earned from my mother with temporary work, which offered me the flexibility to travel. However, after a couple of years doing that, I decided that I'd had a long enough break from corporate America and needed to get back into the rat race. I missed being challenged. I had a bachelor's degree in business and wasn't using it to the best of my ability. The only thing was that I didn't want to be underemployed because of the jobs that I'd taken while I figured out what I really wanted to do. I thought getting a Master of Business would be good for me. It would get me thinking like a businesswoman again. It would be challenging and would bring me current—make me relevant again. But it would take me about two years to get a degree. Could I put off my dream of living in Paris another two years to get a master's in the States? I didn't think so. I needed to figure out how I could do both—live in Paris and get my MBA.

One day I went to the library looking for anything that could help me figure out how to get to Paris and I stumbled upon a book entitled "The Grown-up's Guide to Living in France." It was written for retirees and listed several things you could do in Paris if you retired there—one of which was earn a degree. The author mentioned a few schools that were fully accredited American schools where you could get federal and private loans. It was perfect! I wouldn't have to have $20,000 in the bank or a job lined up in Paris in order to get a visa. I would be a student which meant I'd get a student visa and have my student loan for my essentials. It was the perfect mix of business and pleasure.

Chez Moi

When I relocated to Paris for graduate school, I was scheduled to leave at the end of December 2004 so that I could be in Paris to ring in the New Year, something I'd never done before. But I had to delay my plans because my uncle, my mother's only brother, died suddenly on Christmas day. He died of a pulmonary embolism, the same thing that had killed my maternal grandmother. I didn't wind up leaving for Paris until January 5th after we laid him to rest.

The day I was to leave for Paris I still hadn't figured out where I was going to stay. I was in the shower when my friend, Percy, called. He was the owner and chef at Percy's Place. Percy's Place was one of the few African American owned restaurants in Paris. It wasn't a very big restaurant but it was very quaint and welcoming. And the food was to die for. You could get fried chicken and red beans and rice at Percy's Place, but Percy insisted that his restaurant wasn't a soul food restaurant. He was a professionally trained chef and didn't want to be pigeonholed so there were traditional French entrées on the menu as well. Percy's Place would have gospel brunches on Sundays where my mother sang on occasion. She said that one time she sang so well that one of Percy's patrons was standing on his chair cheering. That just goes to show you how at home Percy made you feel. Unfortunately, I didn't make that trip with her.

Percy called to tell me that he had a friend who was going to be traveling for a few weeks so I could rent his apartment. I was so relieved. That took a lot a stress off my back. I could stay in his apartment instead of spending a lot of money on a hotel and I could take my time finding a place that I really liked.

Paris is made up of twenty *arrondissements* or districts that start with number one in the heart of Paris and then spiral like a snail shell or cinnamon roll to number twenty which is on the border of the city. The apartment I was renting was located in the ninth *arrondissement* just a few blocks from *Pigalle*, the sex district, and one block from where the classical composer, Richard Wagner, once lived. Paris was very good about putting signs on buildings that marked where famous people had resided.

I was very grateful for the apartment but it was one of those places that could only be romantic in Paris. It had one of those old, spiral staircases you see in Parisian buildings which was cool. However, it was on the sixth floor, which would be the seventh floor in the U.S., and there wasn't an elevator. There also wasn't a phone or television and the tub was about the size of a washbasin that my grandma might have washed clothes in once upon a time. It did, however, have a view of the Eiffel Tower. Well...sort of. It was the very tip top of the Eiffel Tower, which I probably wouldn't have noticed if it weren't for its spotlight that shone at night.

Some other things I noticed about my new digs was a sign on the wall that reminded me of something made in a wood shop class in my high school. I never took the class but had friends who had and the projects they worked on looked a lot like this sign. The sign was an address marker and the funny thing was that my high school was on 23rd Avenue and the address on this sign was 26th Avenue. I thought that was interesting but I'm sure there are plenty of 26th Avenues in America. But as I looked at the pictures the owner of the place had on display I saw one of him at a Seattle Mariners game, which was evident by the stadium and the baseball cap he was wearing. Next I noticed memorabilia from Ivar's restaurant on his bookshelf— a famous seafood house in Seattle. I was pretty sure I was in someone's house who was from my hometown.

I asked Percy the name of the owner of the apartment I was renting. It turns out that the owner had attended high school with my uncle. My mom, her siblings, and I all attended Garfield High School in the central area of Seattle. The guy whose apartment I was renting knew my late uncle. I couldn't believe I'd flown thousands of miles to a foreign country and wound up renting a place from someone who came from my hometown and knew my uncle who had passed just days before. Small world! I credit my uncle for being my little angel and getting me a place to stay.

The apartment was a godsend but luckily I didn't have to stay there for long. I preferred to live someplace where I didn't hear drunk couples arguing at night on their way home from *Pigalle*. However, on a vain and positive note, my legs got really toned from going up and down the stairs, even though I tried to go up and down them as little as possible. If I went to the store and forgot something it would usually have to wait until the next time I had to leave.

About a month and a half after arriving in Paris I found my own apartment. I'd originally wanted to live in the seventh *arrondissement*. The seventh is known as one of the most chic districts in Paris. It was the *arrondissement* our hotel was in when I first visited Paris and it was close to the Eiffel Tower. I loved to go to *La Terrasse* restaurant on *Avenue Bosquet*, have their *crème brulée* and people watch, or have a crêpe with Nutella and Grand Marnier at my favorite *crêperie* just around the corner on *Rue Cler*.

One day I wandered into a real estate agency in the seventh and told the agent, whose name was Frank, that I wanted to live in the area. I told him all of the things that I wanted—a full-size bath and kitchen, elevator, washer and dryer, and close proximity to my school. He proceeded to tell me that I didn't want to live in the seventh because I wouldn't get very much for my money. He said he had a really nice apartment that I would like in the sixteenth near *Avenue Marceau*. It was 900 euros per month (about $1,200 U.S.), which was more than I'd wanted to spend but I thought it wouldn't hurt to look. Who was I kidding? I knew if I looked and liked what I saw it would be very hard to resist. But I justified seeing it by telling myself that I hadn't been with an agent before so if nothing else it would be nice for him to get a sense of my taste.

I got in Frank's luxury car, a model that I'd never seen before in the States and he drove me to see the apartment. We crossed the *Seine River* via *Pont de l'Alma* where my favorite Paris tour, *Bateaux Mouches*, is located. The Eiffel Tower was in clear view as we crossed the bridge and continued to the Right Bank and up *Avenue Marceau*. I realized that I had been on a bus ride on that street a couple of years prior with my mother and had wondered what kind of people lived in that area. I saw signs for Yves

Saint Laurent and L'Oréal and it was a stone's throw from the Four Seasons Hotel George V, the *Champs Élysées*, and *Avenue Montaigne*, a street with nothing but luxury stores. Little did I know, when I was riding the bus up *Avenue Marceau* wondering who had the privilege of living in this area, that I'd be living in that same area.

The apartment was very nice. It was furnished, not immaculately but had everything I needed. It had previously belonged to a doctor who saw patients there so there was a video doorbell installed so I could see who was ringing my doorbell and even open my apartment door with the push of a button. The bathroom was very contemporary. It had granite counters, a full-size tub with the customary handheld showerhead that I loved (I never met a shower in Europe that didn't have the handheld showerhead. It's the best thing since the bidet. It lets you get water to places those stationary showerheads don't, if you get my drift. You just feel fresher). The kitchen was small but was an actual kitchen and not a kitchenette, although it only had a half fridge, which is not unusual in Europe. In the kitchen was also an all in one washer/dryer and an oven that could both cook and act as a microwave. The living/dining area had a sleek, built-in, black, mirrored buffet. It also had museum style picture hanging rods that allow you to hang pictures without damaging the walls. A *cave* or storage unit in the basement of the building came with the apartment. I thought about making it a wine cellar but never did.

The apartment was more modern than I'd imagined my apartment would look but was totally me. It was a lot more than I was looking for but right up my alley. I was a graduate student so I wasn't interested in living like a pauper. That was so undergrad! I also knew that I needed certain things in order to make the most out of my trip. I wouldn't be happy if I couldn't have a bath every now and then or had to spend my time dragging clothes to the laundromat and waiting for them to finish instead of doing something fabulous and fun. I wanted to be able to entertain, be close to the action not in the outskirts somewhere, and be able to get to school easily. This apartment had everything that I wanted. I decided to do a little give and take with my budget and get the apartment. *Pourquoi pas?* It wasn't bad for an apartment in one of the most glamorous cities in the world. I reasoned that I'd have paid as much, if not more, for an apartment in New York City. Besides I didn't want to keep looking. If you think it's exhausting looking for an apartment in the States, try looking for one where you are linguistically challenged.

Mes Amies

The bus that took me to school picked me up right on *Avenue Marceau* and dropped me within two blocks of school. It drove me across the Seine past the Eiffel Tower into the fifteenth *arrondissement*. School was interesting because there were people from all over the world: China, Kenya, Nigeria, India, Syria, Lebanon. You name it, we probably had someone from there or nearby. Before going to Paris, I didn't think that I'd have such close friendships with my classmates. I thought I'd really have to network to find friends. To my surprise most of my time would be spent with my classmates or *colleagues* as they call them in France.

My friend and fellow business major, David, helped me move into my apartment. What a nice guy to carry my things (which were plentiful) down seven flights of stairs and taxi them across town to my new place! David introduced me to his girlfriend, Cynthia, who happened to live just about three blocks away from me. It took me a little while to warm up to her. She was loud. I always heard her before I saw her. In the beginning, I needed a few glasses of wine before I could tolerate her. But we grew to be very close, partly because of David and partly because we lived so near each other. All I had to do was walk toward *L'Arc de Triomphe* and in moments I'd arrive at her apartment. We wound up having many dinners at each other's apartments or *Comptoir de L'Arc* around the corner from her place (I absolutely loved their *confit du canard*—roast duck), or our favorite spot off the *Champs Élysées*, Impala Lounge where I'd order kangaroo when it was available. Impala Lounge was an African lounge with great ambiance. On Thursday nights they had live African music. The promoter who brought my mom to Paris, actually managed the music and knew the owners of several clubs in Paris so that usually got me VIP treatment. At Impala Lounge, Cynthia and I would order a *demi-bouteille* (half bottle) or two of the least expensive wine on the menu (it was the most cost effective for our college budgets) and just talk and feel the music. When the live music was over, there'd be a DJ and sometimes a guy playing the congas over the African club music. People danced at their tables, having a good old time. I liked the mix of people. They were what the French would call *bon chic, bon genre* or good style, good sort. They were from all over the globe. It was so cosmopolitan. But what Cynthia and I really loved about Impala Lounge was how close it was to both of our apartments. We could drink as much as we wanted when our budgets allowed and then walk home (sometimes arm in arm to help us walk straight). I loved the fact that I never had to worry about drinking and driving in Paris. Drinking and walking? That was a challenge sometimes.

I first saw my other friend, Rebecca, on registration day. She enrolled a semester or two after me. My first impression of

Rebecca was that she was a little stuffy and strictly business. She was in the registrar's office holding her clipboard close to her chest, wearing eyeglasses, and donning a scarf which screamed "I'm trying to do the French thing!" I didn't know what to think of her but I knew she meant business so I was proud to find out she was a fellow Seattleite. It was nice having someone in Paris from my hometown. It turned out that Rebecca did have a fun side. She and I became fast friends and visited several countries together—Germany, Italy, England, Spain, Belgium, and parts of France.

One of my other BFFs was Caryn. Caryn's reputation preceded her. I kept hearing about this very pretty, black girl from Dallas who was transferring from the London campus. She was a former Dallas Cowboys Cheerleader and a business major like me. The memory most embedded in my mind of Caryn was from my Super Bowl party. The Seattle Seahawks had made it to the Super Bowl. The game was going to be televised live in Paris for the first time and I wasn't about to miss an opportunity to have a party. It's not every day that the Seahawks make it to the Super Bowl. The game would start around three p.m. PST which meant midnight in Paris. Caryn lived in the eighteenth *arrondissement* so she'd stay the night since the metro stopped running at two a.m. I hadn't really spent much time with Caryn before that. In the morning she was the last one to leave my apartment and I got the impression that she hadn't seen another black girl or someone in her age group in a while. She wasn't in any hurry to go home. We talked and talked for hours even though I should have been studying for a test. We shared funny stories about dating. Caryn had dated men of different races. Me? I'd never branched out. We agreed that the black men in Paris made you appreciate African American men. Our brothas keep their hair cut, wear stylish clothes, and have a *"je ne sais quoi"*—A little swagger that you don't see in black men in Paris. The black men we saw, mostly of African and West Indian decent, were either bouncers or street sweepers and weren't the most dapper. This may have something to do with the lack of opportunity for black men in France. People always asked me if I had a fling in Paris and the answer is no. I was divorced and not looking for "Mr. Right Now." If I had been, the bouncers and street sweepers would have sufficed.

Being with Caryn was like being with family. We had a lot in common. Caryn was a few months younger than me (most of our classmates were under thirty), understood my hair and dating issues, and she lived in Dallas where I had family and had spent some time. The one thing that I liked about Caryn was that she was someone that I felt could sharpen me. She was classy, kept herself in good shape, and didn't overdo it when it came to eating and drinking like I did. I felt like she was someone who could be a positive influence in my life.

Serena was another friend that was my age. We met in French class at the Sorbonne. Serena lives in "SoCal" as she would always call Southern California when asked where she's from. We had a lot of fun times together but my most memorable time with Serena was when she broke her nose at my apartment. I'd invited Serena and two girls from school, Kate and Raquel, over to watch a movie. Serena didn't know Kate and Raquel but since I thought they'd get along I invited all of them over to watch Audrey Tautou in *Un Long Dimanche de Fiançailles* (*A Very Long Engagement*). I'd gotten the French version so that we could sharpen our ear for the language. I popped popcorn on the stove and we had drinks *sans alcool*.

My apartment had a mirrored pocket door that could close off the living area from the foyer, kitchen, and bathroom. It was a pretty small apartment so I can't imagine when you would need to use the door but I just *had* to use it. It looked sexy and it was there and I thought this was the perfect occasion. I wanted to make it dark in the living room but I also wanted to make sure that no one would disturb us with the light if they needed to go to the restroom. So I left the entry light on and closed the pocket door but left it open slightly.

Serena is high energy. She's an avid runner and now I see why. It lets her expend some of that energy. Halfway through the film she had to go to the restroom. Having just met Kate and Raquel she was a little nervous and didn't want to hold up the movie too long so she ran full speed to the bathroom. She ran so fast that she didn't see the mirrored pocket door. She hit that door like a bug on a windshield. Splat! I saw and heard her hit the door and then she said, "Oh my God!" and grabbed her nose. Blood was just pouring out of her nose like she had severed a major artery. When she ran into the bathroom blood sprayed onto my mirror and all over the counter. I remember she was wearing an ivory sweater and there was blood all down the sleeve. So much blood was coming from her nose that I thought she was going to die but she didn't want to go to the hospital.

Ironically, we'd remarked shortly before Serena's accident that there was a surprising amount of blood in the movie. Shortly after that the scene in my apartment looked as gory as the scenes in the movie. That's not all. Seeing all of the blood caused Kate to throw up in the popcorn bowl. I was totally surprised because she always seemed like the calm under pressure type but she folded at the sight of so much blood. Raquel was laughing hysterically because she couldn't believe that all of this was happening in tandem. It was just chaotic. Needless to say party over. Kate and Raquel went home and Serena stayed over with an ice pack on her nose. We can laugh about it now.

V.I.P.

Caryn, Rebecca, and I decided to go to Barcelona on our fall break. One place on our list of sights was *Las Ramblas* and the Christopher Columbus monument at the Barcelona harbor. *Las Ramblas* is a long street with shops, street performers, and restaurants that leads to the harbor. We strolled down *Las Ramblas* and when we got to the harbor Caryn needed to go to the ladies' room. She walked off toward a mall or arena to find a public restroom. Rebecca and I stayed back and took pictures.

When Caryn came back she said, "You'll never guess who I ran into. Do you remember Common?"

"The rapper?" I said

"Yes!"

"What is he doing here?" I replied.

"Well I was walking to the restroom and I noticed him and I said excuse me are you Common? He said, 'Yes.' He was with one of Kanye West's backup singers. Apparently, Kanye and Common are having a concert here tomorrow night and they said they will get us passes."

"Are you serious?! Oh my God! That's so cool!"

We were all excited but didn't want to get too carried away in case they didn't really call. The backup singer, whose name was Shawn, told Caryn that he'd call her the next day and get our names and have tickets waiting for us. The following day we did our sightseeing and as it was getting later in the day we talked over some scrumptious tapas and sangria about how we didn't think they'd really call. Just as we were letting disappointment set in the phone rang. Caryn gave Shawn our names and we dashed back to the hotel to get cute for the concert.

The last rap concert I'd been to was in high school when Big Daddy Kane and Biz Markie came to Seattle. That would have been the late eighties/early nineties. I love hip hop but I hadn't heard a lot of Kanye's music other than what was being played on the radio. I don't know what I expected but Kanye put on one of the best shows I'd ever seen in person or on television! He's such a great entertainer. He gained a new fan after that concert. It was so much fun. Part of the fun was being a part of his entourage. We waited to go backstage after the concert and there were all kinds of groupies who thought that we had some sort of clout to get them backstage because they saw our passes around our necks. It was pretty comical. We hung out with Shawn and some other people in their dressing room and then we caravanned with them to their hotel so they could change. Next, we stopped by Kanye's hotel. He got in a car behind ours then we headed to a club on a beach in Barcelona. We were escorted in by security and led to the VIP area where there were hors d'oeuvres, bottles of Moet and Grey Goose, and you could order whatever else you wanted to eat or drink.

There were only a handful of people in VIP and I decided to mingle. I was with Caryn and Rebecca every day. It was time to get to know some of the other people in VIP and even say hi to Kanye. I met his DJ, promoter, and manager, and some of the other people who were lucky enough to get behind the velvet rope. Shawn finally introduced us to Kanye and he was very nice. He wanted to know what our favorite part of the show was. All of the show was good but I told him my favorite part was when he'd come out in the crisp, white dress shirt and designer blue jeans. He always dresses so clean and he was looking good. He said, "Yeah, but what song was I doing?" He really wanted to know what we thought about the show. "Touch the Sky" was his last song and the song where he wore the jeans and white shirt.

We only spoke with Kanye briefly. He had a date with him

and I didn't want her to think that I was hitting on her man. But as soon as she went to the restroom I saw an opportunity to get a picture. I walked up to Kanye and slightly flirtatiously said, "Mr. West." Men like it when you address them as mister.

"Yeah. What's up?" he said as he walked toward me.

"Can I have a picture with you before you leave?"

"Sure," he said. "Take it now." Letting me know that I didn't have to wait. Something was wrong with my camera so I had to rely on Rebecca for pictures. I got Rebecca's attention and asked her to take a picture of me and Kanye. She looked a little shocked. She said, "Did you ask him?"

I said, "Yes."

"What did he say?" she asked as we walked back over to Kanye.

"He said yes." I walked up to Kanye and posed with him for the picture but Rebecca didn't have the camera ready. She was still in disbelief that he had said yes and she seemed a little envious. Her main issue was that I'd asked for a picture by myself and not with her and Caryn. After us discussing in front of Kanye whether or not he was okay with me taking a picture with him Kanye finally said, "Take the damn picture!" and she heard it from the horse's mouth. She was kind of pissed at me for the rest of the evening. Later I asked Common for a picture too. This time Rebecca asked someone else to take the picture so that she and Caryn could get in it. Smart thinking and I didn't mind at all.

It was a very serendipitous evening. We had a lot of fun and everyone in Kanye's crew acted like gentlemen. His female backup singer was very cool as well. You hear so many negative stories about musicians but everyone was very respectful and down to earth.

The Most Fabulous Fondue Party

Valentine's Day 2006, Rebecca and I decided we'd pool our resources and throw a ladies only Valentine's dinner. I was known for my fondue parties so it was a natural choice. What's more romantic than fondue?

I love holidays or any reason to celebrate so I wasn't going to let being single stop me from enjoying Valentine's Day. All of us girls were either single or had a boyfriend back in the States. Being in Paris was like being on a retreat in a sense. You were far away from everyone back home so what else would you do on Valentine's Day in a foreign country? Sit at home or be with your man if he was with you. None of us had a man or either he was thousands of miles away so we decided to have a lovely dinner anyway. Why wait until you have a man to have a beautiful dinner on Valentine's Day?

We could have had a coed dinner but we found evenings more fun when guys weren't involved. We tended to want the type of parties that a manly man would find boring and if you invited men you had to make sure they were having a good time. We just wanted to have a fabulous dinner and let our hair down. We knew that everyone invited would love what we were planning.

There were six of us. Caryn had just broken up with her Italian lover; Rebecca had broken up with her boyfriend who was in the States; Cynthia and David didn't celebrate Valentine's Day; Kay, another one of my colleagues, and I were single, and Traci, another colleague, had a fiancé back home in California.

We bought tea lights, red napkins, and some classy paper plates to set the tone. Rebecca did a great job of decorating the place. It was the first time that I saw my apartment in such sexy lighting. Funny since there wasn't a man in sight but it was something we could all appreciate. Sometimes on a typical Valentine's you work so hard to make things right for your significant other that it can take the fun out of it. With us there was no pressure to make sure the evening was perfect and we didn't have to worry about our mate not doing what we deemed satisfactory for the occasion.

Typically, I'd do cheese fondue made with gruyère and white wine but we did seafood fondue for the first time. We bought fish, shrimp, lobster and an assortment of dipping sauces and accompanied them with a salad and steamed potatoes. Of course we had wine—plenty of it. There were always copious amounts of wine on hand at my dinners. Wine was sometimes cheaper than soda or bottled water so I always had a stash. We decided to have two choices for dessert, the usual milk chocolate and Grand Marnier and, for a little something special, white chocolate with *framboise* or raspberry liqueur. I even made *café framboise* (coffee, raspberry liqueur, and cream with a little whipped cream on top).

The different seafood with the dipping sauces was so tantalizing and then to top it off with the white and milk chocolate fondues—it was like lovemaking for the taste buds. Simply divine!

We had a great time and got a little silly. Somehow some whipped cream got on one of the champagne bottles that we emptied over the course of the evening and Rebecca licked it off like a porno star for Traci's video camera. That's as rowdy as it got. A pretty tame evening but one we all said was hands down our best Valentine's Day. I had other fondue parties after that but there was just no topping our Valentine's fondue.

Bon Anniversaire

For my 33rd birthday (April 13, 2006) I wanted to go to St. Tropez. I'd been before but only long enough to visit the *Musée de l'Annonciade*. Before I'd ever gone to France I was watching television in my room at my parents' house and I came across a channel that was showcasing the art at the museum. At the time I didn't know anything about St. Tropez. All I knew was that the museum had beautiful art and it was located there—a tranquil, port city from what I could see from the show. I was mesmerized by the beautiful, vibrant paintings by Signac and Matisse. I thought that very night that I wanted to go to that museum one day. I didn't know what good reason I'd have to go to St. Tropez but I felt like it was possible. I was naïve to the fact that it was the playground for the uber rich. Not that I would have let that stop me.

My first trip to St. Tropez was alone. I took a bus tour of the French Riviera and we stopped in St. Tropez for a couple of hours. The first thing I did was head for the museum. It was surreal to actually be standing in a place so far from home that I'd only learned of by watching TV and, as a result, dreamed of visiting. The museum was beautiful and St. Tropez was very quaint and welcoming.

I wanted to go back to St. Tropez and actually spend some time there. I thought my birthday was the perfect time. I'd make this my last big trip before returning to the States. Rebecca, Caryn, and another one of our classmates, Fetima, came along. By this time, I was aware that St. Tropez was "to do." I worked really hard to make this trip happen. I did extensive research and was able to find affordable lodging. We stayed in the cutest tiki right on *Plage de Pampelonne*. *Plage de Pampelonne* is where all of the chic beach lounges and restaurants are, like

Nikki Beach, Club Fifty Five, and *La Voile Rouge*.

The first day we were there was a day or two before my birthday. Caryn and I decided to take a walk down the beach to survey the land. We found the famous clubs and we also saw some butt naked sunbathers. I had heard about the nude sunbathers in St. Tropez but was witnessing it firsthand. One guy's cell phone rang while he was literally letting it all hang out. He stood up to take the call and faced our direction, which was toward the water, as if he was trying to get some privacy. He was stark naked! What kind of privacy could you get?

We also saw a lady who was about two hundred and fifty pounds lying out on the beach in the nude. More power to her, I thought. I hadn't seen many full-figured women in France so for her to have the confidence to be nude was cool. Maybe seeing her nude and some other ladies topless was what inspired me to let my boobies out. The girls and I were taking pictures on the beach on my birthday and I told Fetima to take my picture topless. Thank God for digital cameras. I didn't have to waste money discovering that me going topless was not picturesque. I quickly had her delete the photo and said, "Maybe when I get new boobs I'll try it again." I was joking about one day having the guts to get a boob job. I didn't really think I would ever make good on my statement.

Our first evening in St. Tropez the four of us walked the beach to a place called Zanzibar for dinner. It was a little hut with beach service. They made incredible hamburgers. After we ate, we headed back to our tiki. On the way, we saw people dancing at a lounge and decided to stop in. While we were taking everything in, a song came on that I wanted to know the name of so I went up to the DJ to ask what was playing. I thought he was pretty cute but aside from flirting and getting the name of the song I wanted to find out what was going on in St.

Tropez. DJs always know where the parties are. This DJ's name was Oliver. St. Tropez is so small that Oliver had met most of the famous people who had come there. He seemed most excited about knowing P Diddy or "Pee Dee Dee" as he pronounced it.

Oliver told us that it was one of the biggest weekends in St. Tropez. Apparently, the clubs close down for the winter and there is a big to-do Easter weekend when everyone comes back to St. Tropez to open the clubs. Oliver knew all of the spots. He suggested that we have my birthday dinner at *Café de Paris*, a historic and popular restaurant at the port of St. Tropez. Oliver would be deejaying there that night. We were excited that we now had a connection to St. Tropez nightlife.

Some of the most beautiful yachts were docked in front of the restaurant and it was packed inside and out. We had a lovely dinner and great service since we knew Oliver. I loved having a fine dining experience to music played by a DJ. After dinner we went to a club that Oliver recommended and to our surprise people seemed to have learned we were in town. We sat down next to a guy at the club and he said "we heard you were coming." He wasn't the bouncer or the bartender or anything so it was a little weird. If he had worked there it would have made more sense but he didn't. It was like that the whole weekend, which is not a testament to how fabulous I am and my friends are but to how small St. Tropez is. One night we went to Club VIP for an MTV hosted party. Rebecca decided to stay in the tiki that night. When we got to the door of the club, the greeter said, "We were expecting you. Oh I see one of you is missing." We asked each other, how did they know that? I guess there are only a few places you can go on certain nights and, since Oliver was a DJ, word probably got around in the club scene that four American girls had come to party in St. Tropez for the long weekend.

Another night we went to *Les Caves de Roy* for its reopening. It was packed and the DJ was calling out all of the countries of the people that he recognized in the club. He hadn't called out *"Les États Unis"* so I made sure to let him know that we were representin' the United States. *Les Caves de Roy's* VIP section was packed. I spotted Ivana Trump in there sporting a rock on her finger so big that you could see it sparkle in the dimly lit club. I'd seen on a television show that she had a beautiful, namesake yacht and spends quite a bit of time in St. Tropez. She was with a handsome younger man. I ain't mad at her though. Men have been going out with younger women for years. Kudos to her!

One thing I couldn't help but notice at all the clubs I went to in St. Tropez was that no one ordered a 750 ml bottle of champagne. Every champagne bucket you saw had a magnum-sized bottle in it, which is equivalent to two champagne bottles. St. Tropez is one of those places that people with money go to flaunt it. It's a hedonist's heaven. If you have to ask how much something costs you're probably out of your league. That being said, after a little dancing I was thirsty so I went up to the bar and ordered a bottle of Perrier.

"Un Perrier, s'il vous lait," I said.

Being in St. Tropez, all kinds of thoughts raced through my mind in the time it took for the bartender to serve me my Perrier. *How much would a bottle of Perrier cost in an elite club in St. Tropez?* There was no price list. *If it were pricey, what would be different about the color or size of the bottle? Would it have crystals on it? Or would she pour it into a sexy, expensive glass?* I felt like I'd just rolled the dice.

"Vingt euros," the bartender said as she placed the commonplace green bottle of Perrier on the bar.

Oh my God! Did she just say vingt euros as in twenty euros which was almost twenty-five dollars U.S. for the same damn bottle of Perrier that I could get at my super marché in Paris for a little under two euros? All I knew was that I was thirsty and I wasn't going to go all night with nothing in my hand and I surely was not going to act like I couldn't afford a twenty euro bottle of Perrier. I gave her the twenty euros and might have even tipped her. I reasoned that there was no cover charge to get in and I'd have spent twenty euros on drinks and a cover charge in a Paris club easily. Granted it wasn't alcohol, but I was having my thirst quenched. A twenty euro evening was pretty inexpensive. Besides this was my birthday weekend and I was in St. Tropez. When in St. Tropez....

A Souvenir

I had purchased a ball gown years before I went to Paris. There'd been a clearance sale at a store in our outlet mall in Seattle. I got a silver, satin ball gown with a beaded bodice and matching satin wrap for twenty-five dollars. It was in perfect condition. I didn't know where I would wear it but I figured there was always a company dinner over the holidays or some other occasion. That dress hung in my closet for years until I had the idea to have my mom send it to Paris. I thought it would be a nice memento of my time there to take professional pictures at my favorite places. My parents paid for it as my graduation present. I graduated cum laude and received the International Business Award, which goes to one business student for having exceptional business acumen. (I threw that in so that you would know my stay in Paris wasn't all parties and jet-setting.) I'd made arrangements to have the pictures taken a week before I left but it kept threatening to rain. It was two or three days before my departure when it finally seemed like it would be a clear enough day that worked with both my and my photographer's schedule.

Caryn agreed to be my body girl. She made sure that I looked decent in the photos, no lipstick on the teeth or hair looking crazy. She also carried my essentials (comb, brush, and lipstick). We were scheduled to meet the photographer early in the morning in front of *Hôtel de Crillon* at *Place de la Concorde*. *Hôtel de Crillon* is one of the most opulent hotels in Paris. When my taxi pulled up and I exited wearing my ball gown everyone looked at me like I was some kind of star. The photographer, Laurent, kind of smiled as if he'd never met someone quite as eccentric as me. This was our first meeting. I'd originally wanted a colleague of his to do my photos. He took beautiful photos, particularly wedding photos, which was kind of the same thing I was doing but without the groom. However, he was booked during the timing I wanted so he referred me to Laurent. Laurent and I made small talk to break the ice. He took an instant liking to Caryn and serenaded her with a song that included her name intermittently during my photo shoot. Laurent was tall and slim and wasn't a bad looking French guy if you're into that type. I thought his crush was cute but Caryn wasn't interested. He seemed a little transient to her. Not to mention, I think she had had enough of European men after the Italian guy she dated ended their relationship abruptly by pretending to be sick or dead or something.

For my photo shoot I had a few places that I absolutely had to take pictures in, primarily on *Pont Alexandre III*. It is the most ornate bridge in Paris and my favorite. I love bridges and it is one of the most beautiful ones I've ever seen. Two pillars with gold horses and lions anchor each end, gold cherubim embellish the light post along the bridge, and two mermaids with gold torches adorn the center. If you've ever been to Paris chances are you have seen this bridge. *Hôtel des Invalides* where Napoleon Bonaparte was laid to rest is on one side of the Seine River and the *Grand Palais* is on the other side. Secondly, I had to have a shot with the Eiffel Tower in it. We would go to some other locations but those were the must have shots. From *Hôtel de Crillon*, we headed toward *Jardin des Tuileries* where I took pictures sitting on one of those classic green chairs that are in Parisian parks. After *Jardin des Tuileries* we walked over to *Musée du Louvre*. We thought it would be nice to get a picture with the glass pyramid in the background. But when I started to pose for my picture, a guard stopped us and said that I couldn't have my picture taken because I was a model and all models had to get clearance to have their picture taken in front of *Musée du Louvre*. Laurent, whose French naturally is much better than mine, explained to the guard that I wasn't a model. The guard wasn't buying it. I tried to explain to him while Laurent went inside to get clearance. Nothing doing. We walked away and I was disappointed but also flattered. Me? A model?

We walked to *Quai des Tuileries* and got some shots of me walking along the Seine River. I almost bit it walking in high heels on that cobblestone and looking at the camera instead of where I was placing my stiletto. I was a little stiff when we first started shooting but was starting to get into it when a tour boat full of tourists floated by. They all waved at me and cheered as if they were seeing a real model during a photo shoot. Naturally, I waved back. I didn't want to disappoint my fans. It was pretty funny. From there we went to *Pont des Arts*, which connects *Musée du Louvre* and *Hôtel des Monnaies*. There were gusty winds and by the time we were finishing up at *Pont des Arts* there were random sprinkles. My hair was blowing around and there was nothing Caryn could do for me. We proceeded on to *Pont Alexandre III* and I had my picture taken on the bridge with the Eiffel Tower in the background. After it started to sprinkle a little more we decided to call it a day and walked to a café to look over the photos.

We were sitting in a quaint little Parisian café, me sipping champagne imagining what it would be like to have the affluence or lifestyle that went with my attire. It was an absolutely fabulous day and I have some beautiful mementos of my time in Paris. At first I didn't like the pictures. I don't think they are the prettiest pictures of me. Laurent was more of a landscape photographer, whereas his friend was more of a people photographer. I thought the monuments looked better in the photos than me but as time goes on they grow on me. The more I miss Paris, the prettier they become.

No Regrets

Being so financially strapped I felt two ways about Paris. It was the best of times but having a huge student loan, credit card debt, and not making the salary I was expecting made me think it was foolish. After getting the cancer diagnosis and not knowing how long I had to live made my mind go back to Paris except this time instead of having mixed feelings about it, I was very happy that I was able to go.

Paris was the highlight of my life at that time but, expecting to have a long life ahead of me, I didn't want it to be the pinnacle. However, having a life threatening illness made me think it might have been. Was it worth it? Who knows how long I had on this earth? If my life was winding to an end, I was glad that I'd had those experiences and had been to so many places that I'd always dreamed of seeing. I had fulfilled my dream. If my life did end soon, I wouldn't die saying, "I wish I had…" I'd lived in Paris as if I had one chance to live it up. The cancer diagnosis definitely confirmed to me that it was worth it. I was worth it. Who wants to die wishing that they had lived? Life is about making memories.

Karla's Column

Karla and Her Sister, Teressa | Château de Versailles

Valentine's Dinner | Karla's Apartment in Paris

CHAPTER SIX:
Boobs & Bells

*"Faith does not mean trusting God
to stop the storm, but trusting Him
to strengthen us as we walk."*

– Unknown

*M*y mastectomy was scheduled for October 25th, which happens to be my eldest sister, Teressa's, birthday. Ironically, my mother had had her hip replaced on her birthday the previous year. So this was the second year in a row that my sister would have to spend her birthday hoping nothing tragic happened that would forever ruin her birthday. She'd told me not to schedule my surgery on her birthday but I didn't have many options.

Maybe it wasn't the best day of the month to have my mastectomy but if you're going to battle breast cancer, October is the best time to do it. There's so much information available about breast cancer in honor of Breast Cancer Awareness Month. Everywhere I looked I saw pink. Just about every day there was something in the news or on television about breast cancer. My cable company had on demand shows that addressed various facets of breast cancer and breast health.

A few days prior to my surgery, my client was participating in the City of Hope Breast Cancer Walk. Ironically, when the City of Hope came to the office for orientation I wasn't there because I was having my mammogram. I'd never participated in a breast cancer walk and wasn't too keen on doing this one until Jamal talked me into it. It just wasn't my thing. I'd have much rather attended a benefit gala, dinner, or cocktail hour. The walks were starting to seem cliché to me. I couldn't see how it was helping. So many women were still dying of breast cancer in spite of all the money that had been raised over the years. It wasn't until Jamal convinced me that I was benefitting from all of this increased attention given to breast cancer that I decided to walk. I might not have been so vigilant had I not known what to look for by watching television, reading magazines, etc. I raised close to $1,000 and walked in memory of my grandmother and Jamal walked in honor of me.

Naturally, leading up to my surgery, I'd been on the Internet watching every show that dealt with breast augmentations or reconstructions to educate myself about the decisions I needed to make about my own reconstruction. Dr. Kendrick gave me the names of three plastic surgeons she worked with. I asked her to tell me her top two and I made consultation appointments with them. One was a woman, Dr. Murphy, and the other was a man, Dr. Galani.

I had my consultation with Dr. Murphy first. Her office was very well decorated with fresh flowers and a soothing yellow on the walls. When I entered her office, right away I felt like I was in a classy, professional space. There was nothing clinical about the place. Her receptionist was attractive in the way you'd expect someone to look who is the face of a plastic surgeon's office. She took me to a private room where I watched a video of what to expect after a mastectomy and reconstructive surgery and shortly after Dr. Murphy came in. She was a petite woman who wasn't particularly attractive. Her dishwater blonde hair made her appear a little washed out; it was just straight and lifeless no layers, no highlights. She had a rather large, protruding mole on her face that made me wonder why she hadn't done something about it. If you saw her and didn't know she was a plastic surgeon you'd never associate her with beauty. Somehow, I can't get around appearances. I think it must stem from my mother always telling me to look like a lady or to look and dress a certain way for a job or at church (I'm laughing now thinking about how my mom always said "young ladies don't behave like" this or that or "sit like a young lady" if I was in a dress and my knees weren't touching), or maybe my tendency to prejudge is rooted in the simple fact that you wouldn't go to a dentist who had bad teeth. If they don't take care of their own teeth why would they take care of yours?

Dr. Murphy and I talked about my surgery options and she told me she could do a procedure that would allow me to leave the hospital after my mastectomy with my reconstruction completed. It wouldn't involve as much reconstruction as I wanted though. It would have been more of a removal of breast tissue and replacing it with an implant. With the changes I'd seen in my skin (the peau d'orange and swelling of my nipple), I didn't want to just remove breast tissue. I wanted the skin removed as well. She had another procedure that required the use of cadaver skin to replace the skin that I'd lose. Using the cadaver skin was a relatively new technique. I thought it was cool but wasn't too sure how I felt about having some dead person's skin on my breast.

I told Dr. Murphy that I wanted to go a cup size larger and she told me that it wasn't worth it for me to go through the process of adding an expander and waiting for my skin to stretch just to go up one cup size. It sounded like she wasn't going to give me what I wanted but I asked to see photos of her work just to make sure I wasn't passing on someone really good. She brought out two albums of reconstructive surgeries. Up to that point I'd seen pictures online and thought I had a pretty good idea of what the end result of my reconstruction would look like. But when I saw her photos they seemed different, more realistic, more raw and clinical. She wasn't the type of surgeon who would take your previously droopy breasts and give you perky ones. She was the type of surgeon for people who wanted their old breasts back or none at all. I saw pictures of what she could do for me if I didn't want reconstruction, which was very eye-opening. A few of her patients had double mastectomies without reconstruction and in that case she tried to make the scars as appealing as possible. They looked like the smiles on happy faces. I never thought a woman would want both of her breasts removed and not have reconstruction. The only women I'd ever heard of who didn't want breasts were women who wanted to be men. Surprisingly, there *are* women out there who choose not to have reconstruction. Some get prostheses and others just go without. To each her own. There are even some medical conditions that can make one ineligible for reconstruction. Thank God I wasn't in that situation. I had to have my breast removed but at least I could have reconstruction if I wanted. Things could always be worse.

After meeting with Dr. Murphy, I decided that I wasn't the demographic for her. I was a young woman and I wanted young looking breasts and an improvement on what I had. I didn't want my old breast back. They could keep it. And I wanted the right one to get a lift.

My consultation with Dr. Galani was the polar opposite of my consultation with Dr. Murphy. His office was nothing to write home about and his receptionist needed a makeover. Dr. Galani wasn't the most personable person but he was known for giving porn star like breasts. My first impression of Dr. Galani was that he was very concerned about his appearance. He was a handsome, older, Egyptian man. He'd been featured in various Bay Area magazines where he was usually pictured in a nice suit looking very dapper. When he came into the examination room and looked at my breasts he said, "So your right breast is a small C and your left breast is a full B." I was very impressed that he knew that just from looking at me. *This man has seen his share of titties!* I thought. I told him that I wanted to go a little bigger and I wanted perky breasts so that I wouldn't have to wear a bra. "Yes, they will be perky. You will not need a bra." he said with his Egyptian accent and I was sold. *This man gets it*, I said to myself. He suggested that I have reconstruction with an expander as opposed to the flap procedure. The flap procedure, which involves taking skin from your back or abdomen and using it to build the breast(s), was pretty major surgery, would require a week's stay in the hospital, and leave a scar on my back. I didn't have enough belly fat so I would have to pass on the procedure that would take skin from my stomach and allow me to have a free tummy tuck. Dr. Galani thought I was too young to have such a drastic surgery and he was concerned about leaving a scar on my back. All of this, the cancer diagnosis and surgery options, was just thrown at me. I didn't have much time to soak it all in. My main concern was time off of work and cost. Those were a couple of reasons Dr. Galani and I thought it would be best to do the expander procedure.

He would join Dr. Kendrick in the operating room. After she removed my tumor and breast tissue he would come behind her and insert the expander. Once I was healed and before radiation treatment he would add saline to the expander periodically to stretch my skin in preparation for the implant. Radiation makes the skin less porous which makes it more difficult to stretch. It also will harden an implant so I'd have surgery after radiation to swap the expander for a saline implant and do a lift on the right breast. I chose saline implants because of all the bad things I'd heard about silicone. Silicone is FDA approved now but I didn't want one more thing to worry about in addition to cancer. Dr. Galani thought I'd have a better look and feel with silicone but he understood my concerns.

October was a busy month for me in more ways than one. About a week before my surgery Jamal and I decided to elope. He'd been offered the job in Stockton and had been by my side since his interview. Both of our families were happy that we were back together and I'd have Jamal for support. Jamal and I knew we wanted to be married again but we weren't sure how we were going to do it. We didn't want to wait until after my surgery and treatment because tomorrow wasn't promised and we weren't sure how long all of this would take. So we decided that we'd sneak away to Reno, just a two hour drive from Dublin. We hadn't worked out all of our kinks yet. Jamal got really drunk on one of our date nights. He said it was because he was excited to be with me but it let me know that he clearly didn't have his drinking under control. However, he said he was committed to making the marriage work. I was a little nervous about what he'd be like in a casino since in our previous marriage he'd been a little excessive when it came to gambling. Being in Reno would be a test of sorts.

We'd gone all out for our first wedding. We didn't need all

of the fanfare this time. Been there. Done that. The second time around we had the wedding that people I envied had. For me, everything had to be so extravagant. I couldn't do anything small or low key. I remember Jamal and I toyed with having our first wedding in Jamaica where we were having our honeymoon because my parents said they couldn't afford to pay for the wedding. It wasn't ideal but I was willing to do it if push came to shove. But my parents came through and Jamal covered a large part of the cost. We didn't have to elope that time and after it was all said and done, it was the most wonderful day of my life. However, although I thought the wedding was beautiful, it was a lot of work and we probably should have used the money for a down payment on a house instead. On our honeymoon we saw a couple who had just gotten married on the island—the groom still in his tuxedo and the bride still in her gown—and we thought it didn't look half bad.

When we got home from our honeymoon, someone had set up our apartment cabana and pool area for a wedding and it looked so elegant. I thought, *Why couldn't I do something like that?* This time around I would. I was going to have a no muss, no fuss wedding. I didn't even buy a new outfit. I tried but I didn't find anything that I really liked. We didn't buy new rings either. We both still had our original wedding rings, which was really special. We hadn't gotten our wear out of them anyway. We'd only been married the first time for four years, three of which were spent apart.

Once we checked into our hotel we went down to the casino. It was interesting because neither of us had "the fever." We only spent a short time down there (definitely not what would have happened in marriage number one) and then went to one of the restaurants to have dinner. We sat at the bar which was customary when I went out to eat with Jamal. He had to be at the bar. You get your drinks quicker there. Somehow at the end of our dinner we got into an argument right there in the restaurant (definitely reminiscent of marriage number one). I remember it was brought on by Jamal's drinking but I don't remember what the fight was about. It was always possible to have some sort of misunderstanding when he'd had too much to drink. The argument could have been that I told him to slow down on the drinks or maybe I asked him how much he'd tipped or maybe I was too friendly to the guy sitting next to me at the bar. All things we'd argued about before but I can't remember what this fight was about. I do remember that we argued all the way back to the room and I was in tears and was seriously considering not going through with the wedding.

"I don't know if I want to do this." I told Jamal as I sobbed on the bed. This relationship was feeling too similar to the one we had before. I felt like I was seeing what our future would be like. Hearing me say I didn't want to go through with it made Jamal calm down. He became more serious and looked at me and said, "I love you and I want to marry you." All I could do was think about the dysfunction that I was experiencing and how this might not be a good idea. I also thought about what would happen if I didn't marry him. I would be going through this cancer battle in California by myself. I'm sure my family would come up when they could but it would be a huge inconvenience.

I was crying and thinking what a negative way this was to go into a marriage. Jamal said "Karla, what are we going to do?" It was getting late and the wedding chapels were going to close soon so I needed to make a decision. I'd never seen Jamal look the way he did. I could see in his eyes that he was really worried that I might not marry him. That look told me that he really wanted this and would do whatever he had to do to keep me.

I decided to go through with the wedding. "Okay. I'm okay." We kissed and made up and I grabbed the phone book to find a chapel.

Looking at all of the quickie wedding spots made us laugh a little which helped lighten the mood. We decided that we'd get married at The Chapel of Love. They were open late and had the best price. We were going to do a drive thru wedding but their drive-thru was closed. We got a kick out of how low budget and sans fanfare we were going this time around.

Entering the Chapel of Love was like entering a time machine. It reminded me of my grandparents' home in pictures I'd seen. The furniture looked like it was from the fifties and they had little knickknacks for sale that had probably been on the shelf for as long as I am old. There were old garters, cake toppers, figurines, and dolls.

Jamal and I sat in the waiting area marveling at all of the kitschy souvenirs while waiting for a couple ahead of us to be done with their ceremony. They were a cute young couple who you could tell had gotten new clothes for the occasion. They were both in black and white. It was so sweet that they were standing with each other having this very private and intimate moment. I wondered why they were there alone. *What was their story? Why had they come to the Chapel of Love? Was she pregnant? Did one of their parents not agree with their union so they'd come to Reno instead of having a formal wedding?* Judging a book by its cover, I gathered that they were mature and responsible for their age. This marriage was very intentional and it looked like they were taking it seriously. I said a silent prayer that God would bless their marriage.

The longer I sat there witnessing the atmosphere of love, the better I felt about me and Jamal recommitting our lives to each other. When it was our turn, one of the staff took us into the chapel. The lights were low but there was pink and purple mood lighting and there were fake flowers adorning the altar. Rev. Flint (whose name reminded me of Larry Flynt, the creator of Hustler magazine, which made the Chapel of Love feel even more cheesy) presided over the ten to fifteen minute ceremony. Jamal and I held hands and looked into each other's eyes as we recited our vows. The first time we recited our vows I don't think we ever really thought we would have to deal with bad times, sickness, or "until death do us part." I was only twenty-four and Jamal twenty-seven. But this time those words took on a deeper meaning and significance. When I got to the part about "in sickness and in health" that was the crack in the proverbial dam. Tears started flowing like someone had opened the floodgates. I was overcome knowing what I was about to endure and knowing that Jamal was marrying me in spite of me being sick, getting ready to lose one breast, and death possibly parting us a lot sooner than either of us had hoped. Jamal wiped my tears and when we were done reciting our vows we kissed and became husband and wife for the second time. I was Mrs. Mitchell again. We didn't take any pictures, which in hindsight makes it even more special. It's a memory that only the two of us share and as cheesy as the Chapel of Love sounds it was very romantic that night.

CHAPTER SEVEN:
Young & Breastless

"You never know how strong you are until being strong is the only choice you have."

– Cayla Mills

I was diagnosed with breast cancer in September of 2007. That was definitely a September "issue" but there was another September issue that I had—*Vogue* Magazine's September issue. On my last visit to Dr. Kendrick's office I picked up the biggest *Vogue* magazine I'd ever seen. *Vogue* touted it as their "biggest issue ever— 840 pages of fearless fashion." This issue was equivalent to the JCPenney or Sears Christmas catalogs I waited so anxiously for during the holidays as a child. I, like most kids, would look through the catalog and put my initials next to the things I wanted. This issue of *Vogue* was the Christmas catalog all grown up.

Dr. Kendrick's receptionist saw how much I loved it and gave it to me. Reading *Vogue* always transports me to Paris and I thought this magazine would be perfect to read while I recovered from surgery. Since surgery was a few weeks out, my plan was to not look at it again until recovery when I could read it in peace and dream about better days ahead—like me being healthy and wealthy walking down Avenue Montaigne. Instead of walking by the luxury boutiques as I had when I lived in Paris, I would actually be able to stop inside and purchase those designer bags and haute couture that adorn the pages of *Vogue*. Being 840 pages, this magazine would keep me busy for quite a while.

On this particular visit to Dr. Kendrick's office my mother was with me and we decided to go to the Berkeley marina for lunch afterwards. My mother wanted to bring the *Vogue* into the restaurant so that she could look through it. When we got home I asked my mom for the magazine and it was nowhere to be found. We called the restaurant but they said they didn't have it. There were a few people there that looked like they would have loved to have my magazine and they were a little too quick to say they didn't have it. But the restaurant was forty five minutes away from my apartment so I had to take their word for it. My mother vowed to get me another copy but I knew the issue was no longer on store shelves. I was hoping my mother could get her hands on a copy but she's not the most computer savvy and nowadays I knew she'd need to email somebody and maybe even go to Google or *Vogue*'s website.

Karla's Column

On Oct 5, 2007, "Edna" mom@email.com> wrote:

Dear Sir/Madame:

I am desperately trying to locate a copy of the September 2007 issue of your magazine. My daughter who lives in California and was recently diagnosed with breast cancer was given this magazine by her surgeon's reception. Since I was so eager to look at this issue before I left California, I accidentally left it in a restaurant where we stopped for lunch. I have looked everywhere for a copy and hope you sell back issues of this magazine.

Please reply to me as soon as possible because I will be leaving to return to California where my daughter will be having her surgery. She is looking forward to reading it while she is recuperating. Thank you so much.

Miss Edna

P.S. (It is the magazine that says 840 pages, the biggest ever....)

Date: Tue, the 9th Oct 2007

Subject: Re: How to Obtain September, 2007 Issue of Fashion Magazine

From: email@vogue.com

To: mom@email.com

Ms. Baptiste –

The September 2007 issue sold out and there are no copies at the warehouse available for sale.

However, we do have a few extra copies here in our office and since yours is a special case, I would be glad to send you one to take to your daughter. No charge. Send me your full name and address and I'll send it out to you. Since it will take a few days to get to you (unless you live in the New York area) because it will go out at magazine rate, you might want to give me your daughter's address so that I could send it directly to her.

Ms. Richardson

Vogue Information

From: mom@email.com

To: karla@email.com

Subject: FW: How to Obtain September, 2007 Issue of Fashion Magazine

Date: Mon, the 15th Oct 2007

See K.K. God does answer prayer. I am so happy to get this magazine back for you. I was really bothered by losing it. Love Mom

The day before my surgery was very charming and surreal. My parents came to be by my side, my magazine arrived (it was so nice of Ms. Richardson to send me the magazine free of charge, especially since it weighed nearly five pounds. The shipping couldn't have been cheap), and my husband surprised me with a dozen pink long stem roses. He was a little nervous about the surgery and wanted to make sure I saw the flowers before I went under the knife in case I didn't make it out.

There's always a strange energy the day before a major surgery. It's kind of like the energy you feel the night before taking an early morning flight, except in this case you're not excited like you would be if you were taking a trip. You're going on a journey, however. A journey into the unknown and everyone wants to make sure that you know they love you and are thinking of you. I received lots of phone calls from friends and family. It was nice to know that I would have so many people praying for me. That made me feel really good.

To prepare for my little stay *Chez* John Muir (John Muir was the name of my hospital), I packed up my pink button down satin pajamas that I'd purchased for the occasion. I would need clothes that I didn't have to pull over my head since my arm movements would be limited after surgery. (Even though I'm a girly girl, I never really liked pink. I didn't hate it but I didn't really start to embrace it until I had breast cancer. I was a cheerleader in high school so I like to get into the spirit if you will.) I made sure Jamal had the numbers of all of my friends and co-workers who needed to know that I came out of surgery okay. And I packed my little vanity case along with my September issue of *Vogue* and other reading materials since I would be in the hospital for two to three days depending on how quickly I recovered.

We pulled up to the hospital at five in the morning. It was so dark there were still stars in the sky. As I was walking up to the entrance of the hospital my cell rang. It was Serena. "Hi Kar Kar my friend! I just wanted you to know that I am praying for you."

I don't know how she thought to call me at that hour but it was perfect timing. Serena's a devout Catholic. I'm a Protestant so we don't necessarily have identical beliefs. I know she prays to Jesus but she might pray to Mary too. Nonetheless, when you're diagnosed with cancer you don't give a rat's ass who's praying for you or who they're praying to. If a Buddhist says they are going to chant for you, you let them chant. If an atheist says they are going to send good thoughts, you'll be happy to have those thoughts sent to "the Universe." All the religiosity goes out the window. You start to realize that you don't have everything figured out. I didn't have all of the answers and as long as people were unified around the same purpose—my healing—it was all good.

Surprisingly, I wasn't anxious about the surgery. I was actually looking forward to getting the tumor out of my body and, call me strange, but I actually like going under. I've had minor procedures in the past and the best part to me was getting the anesthesia. When they called me back to surgery prep, I stripped down and put on my patient gown, some teds (anti-embolism stockings), and one of my favorite surgery souvenirs-- slipper socks. My favorite surgery things are anesthesia, slipper socks, and warm blankets. *Ahhhhh.* (I'm the type of person who will find something "fabulous" in any occasion.) The anesthesiologist came in and explained to me what was going to go down with the legal drugs they were giving me to make me feel goooood. All of the hospital staff was in scrubs and hospital attire but then Dr. Galani arrived in a perfectly tailored navy pinstripe suit, with a complementary red tie, *and* he was wearing cologne to boot. I was flattered that he'd dressed up for the occasion. He proceeded to pull out his marker and, as if he were a tailor himself, made little marks where he would cut and stitch me. I felt like a canvas and I just prayed that in the end I'd look like a masterpiece. After he'd made his mark so to speak, the nurses wheeled me to the operating room. The anesthesiologist went to work and the last thing I remember is reciting the alphabet in reverse. Z...Y...X...w...v...u...t......

The next thing I remember was I'd come to and could hear everything going on around me but I couldn't move—I couldn't even open my eyes. I had a breathing tube in my throat, which made it difficult for me to breathe. I started to panic, which made me gag and start convulsing. I wanted to yell "HELP!" but I couldn't speak. Dr. Galani and the nurses were just standing around me talking about something insignificant while I thought I was going to suffocate. My convulsions must have alerted them that I needed to have the tube taken out of my throat and someone was nice enough to relieve me. It was a very scary experience.

Other than that, my surgery went well. Dr. Kendrick came to check on me a little while after they took the tube out of my throat. She let me know that she'd removed the entire tumor but they'd found cancer in my sentinel lymph node. The sentinel lymph node is the first lymph node that cancer will likely spread to if it metastasizes. When doctors perform a sentinel node biopsy they pump a blue dye near the tumor which leads them to the sentinel node. If there is cancer in your sentinel lymph node, all of your lymph nodes are removed and tested.

With that news, it looked like I would most likely need to have chemotherapy. I knew it had spread to my lymph nodes. I knew that the technician had seen something the radiologist hadn't seen. I knew my underarm wasn't swelling because it was irritated as Dr. Kendrick had told me. I knew it was swelling because I had cancer in there. *I knew it.*

When it was time for me to leave the hospital, I'd received so many flowers that I needed two carts to get all of them to the car. The hospital sent three teenage girl volunteers to help escort me out—one for each cart and one for my wheel chair. Throughout this whole ordeal I held up pretty well emotionally until they wheeled me out of my room. I could tell when my nurses were saying goodbye to me that they were thinking: *she's so young.* I could see the pity in their eyes. Add to that, girls twenty years my junior without a care in the world wheeling me out, laughing and giggling with each other. Something about it was very poignant and I had to fight the tears. To make matters worse, when we got to the lobby everyone was looking at all of my beautiful flowers and me, being young and being wheeled out of the hospital. The looks on their faces said, *Wow! Somebody must really love her. I wonder what she was here for. She must have had a baby but where's the baby?* I could see the confusion on their faces. I felt mixed emotions being wheeled out of the hospital, which I liken to what I think the emotions of a wounded, one-legged veteran in a Memorial Day parade would be—pride that I'm a fighter, sad that I was wounded in battle, and happy that I'm still standing. It was tough but I succeeded in swallowing my tears that day. I hadn't cried (other than at my wedding) since I'd been diagnosed and I wasn't about to let the tears start now—in front of strangers.

The day after I left the hospital I received a call from Dr. Kendrick. She'd gotten back my tumor and lymph nodes pathology report. Jamal was at work and my parents were taking care of me. When they heard the phone ring they came into my room to see if it was Dr. Kendrick. We were expecting her call. They listened attentively to my side of the conversation, trying to deduce what was being said on the other end. They could tell by the change in my countenance and the tone of my voice that I wasn't getting good news. My parents stood there, hugging and bracing themselves.

My mother whispered anxiously, "What? What is it?"

I start repeating what Dr. Kendrick said. "My tumor was larger than they thought. They thought it was under two centimeters but it was actually four centimeters. They also found cancer in fourteen out of twenty four of my lymph nodes."

My mother turned into my father's chest and started to cry. I immediately gestured for her to leave so she went into the bathroom. She'd been so strong for me up until that time but I didn't want people crying and carrying on, probably because I knew that if they went there I would be soon to follow. It's hard on the cancer patient to see our loved ones breakdown. We don't ever imagine our lives taking this turn so for some of us to see our parents or loved ones grieving makes death seem possible. It makes our mortality even more real. In my situation I felt that, when you open the door to sadness, hopelessness is the next to knock on the door. I was the drum major of this parade, so to speak, and I wasn't changing the tempo for any reason.

Seeing my parents embrace and console each other was sweet. It's not often that they are on the same page. They'd been married forty years at the time and over the years they'd separated once and talked about divorcing numerous times. I'd never seen them as close and united as they were at that moment. They were encouraging each other to stay strong.

I consider my mother a woman of faith. I know she had everyone she knew praying for me. She even had people she didn't know praying for me. She'd met a breast cancer survivor in the grocery store who told her she would add me to her prayer list. So when I got the news that my cancer was worse than I thought, it surprised me when my mom burst into tears. I knew she probably cried when she wasn't with me but to see her cry in front of me so easily let me know that she thought she might lose me. I wasn't ready to think that way.

Dr. Kendrick said she definitely advised me to have chemo but I was still a little reluctant. I felt like they really didn't know the long term effects of chemo for someone in my age group. Why couldn't I take a natural approach? Start juicing, take vitamins, eat green, leafy vegetables? I'd seen the movie "The Secret" and there'd been a lady on there who used positive thoughts and visualized herself cancer-free and had been healed. I wished that I could do that. I believed in the law of attraction somewhat. However, having just received an even worse diagnosis than before I wasn't willing to take any chances with unproven remedies. Dr. Kendrick referred me to an oncologist to have a consultation. I was able to get an appointment two days later.

With my tumor the size it was and with the number of lymph nodes that were cancerous I was now stage III instead of stage II. Before I received the news I'd wondered how far my faith could take me. I thought I could handle stage III and that's it. If I'd had stage IV I thought I wouldn't be able to believe that I'd be healed from that. I'd never heard of anyone surviving stage IV cancer. Stage IV is when the cancer has travelled to other parts of the body, not just your lymph nodes. Stage IV is the beginning of the end in my book, but stage III still had some decent statistics. At the time, according to the American Cancer Society (ACS), 86% of women with stage II breast cancer live beyond five years after diagnosis, 57% of women with stage III, and 20% with stage IV. I could see myself being in the 86% group and even in the 57% group but that 20% group was cutting it close.

To be totally candid, before I had breast cancer, I'd admired survivors of the disease because it seemed like quite an accomplishment. I'd heard people introduce women who were breast cancer survivors at conferences or on TV and because they'd survived breast cancer, people always responded as if the woman had climbed Mt. Everest three times in high heels. I remember thinking *I want to be a breast cancer survivor.* Crazy I know, but it's the truth. However, I never in a million years thought I'd ever be faced with the disease. Certainly not at my age. But when I was, I thought, *stage 0 or stage I is like you didn't even really have cancer. Five years out you have a 100% survival rate. Stage II is bad but you still caught it early. You might even get by without chemotherapy or radiation but not both. Stage III? Now if you go through that you've gone to the brink and back. You're one stage away from the big one. If I'm going to be a breast cancer survivor I want to survive something inspirational. Have a story to tell. A testimony.*

Now that I was diagnosed with breast cancer I saw how ridiculous it was to make such a big deal about someone surviving breast cancer. If you survive breast cancer it is not because of anything that you've done. It's by the grace of God. You can get kudos for having a great attitude while you went through it. But, if there was something that *we* could do to make certain that *we* survived breast cancer, women all over the world would be doing it and we wouldn't need to have breast cancer walks or fundraisers. We would have *the cure*. Quite frankly, if we were so in control we would never have gotten the disease in the first place. Being diagnosed with cancer is and should be a very humbling experience.

Years before I was faced with having a mastectomy, I remember seeing people on television who'd lost limbs but had great attitudes in spite of their losses. It made me wonder how I'd react if I lost a limb. *Would it destroy me?* Seeing these people let me know that it wasn't the end of the world. You could harp on it and be depressed, which is like a life sentence in a self-imposed prison, or you could accept it and live in your new normal. If I lost anything I didn't want it to be a limb but I knew if I lost a body part I'd get through it. I'd also seen a woman on Oprah who couldn't have a child and she was so depressed about and oppressed by it every day. She was miserable. I never wanted to be the type of person who'd be perpetually miserable about something that I couldn't change. I want to be able to surrender to God's will and see what it is He has for me to glean from the experience. I've learned that God is omniscient and He knows what I need before I even know I need it. Having had a few miscarriages I felt that if God doesn't give me any kids there must be a good reason for it and I'll be content. I felt the same way about losing a limb or abilities.

So there I was in my room at home, all bandaged up in my pink polka dot satin pajamas. The brave part of me said, "Stage III? Bring it on!" The scared part of me thought, *Am I going to die soon? Will I survive this? I hope this is the end of the bad news.*

It was four days after my surgery. Jamal was at work and my parents were in the living room. I was in my bedroom and I was curious to see what I looked like without my left breast. I didn't feel like I didn't have a breast because of all of the bandages. Everyone was worried that I'd really take it hard, especially since I'd held up so well so far. They didn't know that I really wasn't all that attached to my breasts. I really saw it as a positive that I'd give my saggy breast and get a perky one in return. I knew it wouldn't feel like a real breast but I figured it would look like one.

I walked over to the full-length mirror in my room and unbuttoned my pajama top. I opened the Velcro closure bra that the hospital had sent me home in and peeked inside my bandages. What I saw was not scary at all. I had a scar where I'd had a nipple and breast but I saw the scar as a battle wound. I was a soldier in the battle against breast cancer and I'd been wounded. I deserved a Purple Heart, only I wouldn't take anything away from the men and women who fight to keep our country safe. I would give myself a pink heart. My scar said that I'd been through something and was still here. I looked at myself in the mirror and I thought I looked beautiful—one breast and all.

The next day Jamal was at work and my parents and I were at the apartment watching television. The phone rang and my mom answered it. I didn't know who it was but I could hear that there was bad news that I was being protected from. I could tell by the conversation that it was one of my in-laws and something had happened to Jamal but I didn't know what. When my mom got off the phone she told me that Jamal had been arrested at work. His former employer had accused him of embezzlement and, not only that, he hadn't cleared up a DUI charge that he'd gotten in Sacramento before he moved to Las Vegas, so they considered him as driving with a suspended license. He was in the Sacramento County Jail. Here I was with bandages on, healing from a mastectomy, and my husband had just been arrested. I couldn't believe it! This was a total shock to me. My parents were very understanding and supportive. We made the two hour drive from Dublin to Sacramento to visit Jamal in jail, find out what was going on, and see how we could get him out. Jamal's parents met us there.

We had to wait what seemed like a light year for Jamal's visiting hour. While we were waiting my mom spotted an attorney who looked like he had a good rapport with the officers so she asked for his card. She figured he must be a good attorney because he seemed like he was no stranger to the place and like he had some clout. At least now we had the name of an attorney who could probably help us. When Jamal's visiting time came, only three of us could go in so my dad and father in-law stayed back. I was totally out of my element. The officers treated us like we knew the routine, as if we visited people in jail regularly. Some of the people who knew the system were nice enough to clue us in. When we got to the wing that Jamal was in, we were to wait outside a door until we heard the buzzer, which meant we could enter the visitation room. Then the "inmate" would come up to the window and talk to us over the phone. Jamal came out in an orange get up that, were it not for the Sacramento County Jail stamped on them, I'd have thought they were scrubs.

I hated seeing him in there because I knew there were a lot of people who deserved to be there but in my mind he wasn't one of them. He wanted us to find him an attorney because he wasn't going to go with a public defender who'd probably want him to take a plea on the embezzlement charge. He wasn't going to plead guilty to something that he hadn't done.

According to Jamal, his former employer, let's call them BS Electric, was trying to accuse him of stealing electrical supplies and selling them. The truth of the matter was that they were mad at him for leaving the company and taking some of their customers with him. There was a police detective who'd kept track of Jamal from Sacramento to Las Vegas and back to California and she seemed like she had a personal vendetta against him. She'd call him at work in Las Vegas and harass him and try to scare him into turning himself in. He would tell her that she couldn't scare him because he knew he was innocent. When she'd arrested him she totally defamed his character by telling his current employer that they should be careful who they hired as she'd taken him out of his office in handcuffs. This was all news to me. Jamal told me about being blacklisted in the industry because of parting ways with BS Electric but I didn't know about any looming legal battle or the DUI.

Naturally, when we saw Jamal he was stressed out. We needed to find him an attorney at a good price because we didn't have a lot of money. We were hoping the one my mother approached at the jail would be affordable. We also needed to come up with the money to bail him out. It was crazy!

So Jamal and I were both in battles—mine life threatening and his character damaging. Somehow I wasn't that worried about my husband being found guilty and being thrown in jail for embezzlement. I knew the Lord hadn't brought us back together to take my husband from me. I felt the same way about my cancer. I felt I would at least have some time with my husband. We'd been married all of ten days when this happened. I knew it was just a test, trying times that we would get through together.

CHAPTER EIGHT:
Preparing to be Poisoned

"That which does not kill us makes us stronger."

--Friedrich Nietzsche

Halloween Day I kept my cell phone close, awaiting news on Jamal as I walked into my first appointment with my oncologist, Dr. Scott. I'll never forget that it was Halloween because Dr. Scott's staff was in costume and there was a lady from another office in the building who stopped by dressed as a kooky French maid. She had on exaggerated makeup and huge butt pads which got a laugh out of my dad. So much so that we took his picture with her. I'd been looking forward to this appointment because until then all I knew was that I had cancer. There wasn't much talk about what we were going to do about it. Other than surgery, we hadn't done anything. I had a breast surgeon and a cosmetic surgeon but I was wondering when I'd see a cancer doctor. Finally, the day had come.

Dr. Scott entered the exam room. She introduced herself to my parents and me and then she held my hand, looked me in the eye and said, "How are you doing?" I said, "Fine." But then she looked deep into my eyes and said, "Really?" and I burst into tears. I didn't know where that had come from but I suppose I needed it considering all that was going on in my life. Dr. Scott told me she had that effect on people. All the talk of *you have cancer, you have cancer, you have cancer* builds up and, until I was actually battling it, I felt anxious. I was finally at the point where I could have an action plan. Not only did I cry, I literally exhaled. My father was very impressed with Dr. Scott. He thought she was very sharp and young enough to have been recently exposed to the latest treatments and trials. I think all of us breathed a sigh of relief when we left there.

Dr. Scott recommended that I have sixteen weeks of chemotherapy; four treatments of Adriamycin a.k.a. "The Red Devil" every other week followed by four treatments of Taxol and Cytoxan one after the other every other week. She said my hair would fall out right after the second treatment and she recommended that I shave my head. It could be traumatizing for some people to see big plugs of their hair coming out. After I'd had a few weeks of recovery from chemotherapy I'd start six weeks of daily radiation. She said my treatment was aggressive but appropriate for my stage. After radiation, she would put me on a drug called Tamoxifen that would turn off my estrogen receptors since my cancer was estrogen fed. I'd have to take it for five years.

Since chemo drugs have so many side effects I'd need to have a consultation with the nurse practitioner to learn what the side effects were and how to manage them. Dr. Scott also recommended that I go on long term disability, which was a shocker to me. I'd heard of people going through chemo and working and so I figured that's what I'd do. I had just started my job so I was concerned about what they might think. Dr. Scott said that she wanted me to take this time to focus on me and healing and she didn't think working would be a good idea. Worries aside, I liked her way of thinking. When I'd had my bout with chronic fatigue and depression years ago I remember the doctor wanted to put me on an anti-depressant. Since I'm medication averse, I didn't want to take it. Plus, he'd said that if I stopped taking it I could wind up even more depressed than when I started. I told him that my body was saying that I needed rest not a pill. I'm sure that's what most people who are on anti-depressants bodies are telling them but they won't slow down. I've never been one of those people that thought work was more important than taking care of myself. I knew that if I croaked they'd find someone else to do my job in a heartbeat. I also know that if I were on my death bed I wouldn't be concerned about work. I couldn't start chemotherapy until my mastectomy wounds had totally healed so I had a little time to let all of this stuff about work sink in. I'd have my chemotherapy consultation in the next few days.

We were able to post bail for Jamal, which made both of us very happy. He'd been so worried about me while he was in there, which is understandable. We also managed to pay the retainer fee for the attorney we'd seen when we visited the jail the first time. Jamal would need to meet with him every so often to bring him up to speed on the background of the allegations. This would mean frequent trips to Sacramento.

Let me remind you that Jamal had been recently hired by his employer and was arrested at work. I'm sure that hadn't left the best impression but thankfully they were willing to take him back. Since he'd be home with me in the evenings, we thought it was a good idea if he didn't take off of work too often to accompany me to chemo or doctor's appointments. Besides, he couldn't drive so he couldn't help me if I couldn't drive because of the treatment side effects.

My parents accompanied me to my chemo consultation. They wanted to know all about what these chemotherapy drugs were going to do to me. My nurse practitioner, Linda, explained all of the side effects that *could* happen during chemotherapy. She said I might not experience them all but she had to tell me about them. I could have low white blood cell counts, which meant I would be more susceptible to colds and infections; low red blood cell counts, which could lead to anemia; low platelet counts, which could prevent my blood from clotting; Leukemia; nausea; vomiting; constipation; diarrhea; damage to the lining of my mouth and throat; darkening of my tongue, palms of my hands, soles of my feet and nail beds; bone, muscle and joint pain; loss of lung function; heart muscle weakness and palpitations; peripheral neuropathy, which is nerve damage that results in increased sensitivity, tingling of the extremities, decreased muscle tone, and loss of balance; headaches; hot flashes; bleeding in my bladder; a metallic taste in the mouth; confusion and depression; my hair would fall out and my nails would detach from the nail beds; and last but certainly not least I could have an allergic reaction, which would be evident by low blood pressure, shortness of breath, chest pressure, hives, itching, or death. Basically, I was thinking, *If the cancer won't kill me, the chemo will.*

Hearing all of this didn't put my fearful mind at ease. I felt like I was in a bad pharmaceutical commercial. Not the beginning when they make everything look rosy because you're taking their drug. The end when the narrator rattles off all of the side effects—some of which make you want to keep your ailment: "May cause anal itching, bad breath, depression, sexual dysfunction, and suicidal thoughts. Call your doctor if you experience sudden weight gain, rectal bleeding, acne, hives, or rash." No thanks!

Linda also explained that it was a good idea for me to have a vascular port implanted in my chest. If I didn't get the port I'd run the risk of my veins collapsing or simply burning out due to the potency of the drugs. A vascular port is a little device that sits underneath your skin that has a catheter that leads to a vein. In my case it would lead to my heart via my superior vena cava. This vein is a lot better suited than the little veins in my arm to take the beating that these drugs were going to give. Having the port would also save time because the nurses wouldn't have to try to find a vein to administer the drugs each session. Linda also said that I needed to have a baseline echocardiogram done prior to starting chemo. That way if I had any trouble with my heart they could do another echocardiogram and compare the two.

I wasn't gung-ho about any of this but I didn't have any better ideas. So we went ahead and scheduled my chemo and other appointments that I needed to have prior to chemo. The scariest test I had was a PET (Positron Emission Tomography) scan for the simple fact that it would scan my entire body to see if the cancer had spread beyond my lymph nodes. Dr. Scott suggested that I have one since so many of my lymph nodes were cancerous. She must have read my mind because I was wondering how they were going to make sure I wasn't worse than we thought with fourteen out of twenty four lymph nodes having cancer. I was glad she was being thorough but at the same time I was a little nervous. Luckily, the PET scan was clear so we definitely knew that I didn't have stage IV breast cancer. That was the best news I'd heard in a while.

Karla's Column

Update

From: Karla (karla@email.com)

Sent: Wednesday, Nov. 14, 2007

Hello Everyone,

I have to apologize for not sending an update sooner. Since my surgery things have been a little hectic. My plan was to have my surgery, recover for a couple of weeks, go back to work, and go through the process of getting my new boobs. :o) However, when my surgeon got back my pathology report they found that my tumor was actually four cm instead of two cm and cancer was in fourteen of twenty four of my lymph nodes as opposed to zero. So that changed my diagnosis from stage II to stage III. Now it is projected that I will be off of work for six months going through chemo and radiation. My parents just went back to Seattle on Saturday. They stayed to hear from my doctors first hand and help Jamal and me with getting me to my appointments that I needed to have before I start chemo.

Needless to say I've been out of my routine and haven't had much time to talk on the phone and email. Not to mention, I'm a newlywed and have been enjoying any peaceful moments I get cuddling with my husband.

I just wanted you all to know that I appreciate your friendship, encouragement, prayers, and cards. Chemo starts on Nov. 28th and I'll have sessions every other week for sixteen weeks followed by six weeks of radiation. I really don't want to do this to my body but I trust that the Lord will bring me through with flying colors. In addition, I want to do all that I can nutritionally to make sure that I reduce my side effects and bounce back.

Keep me in your prayers!

Love,

Karla

CHAPTER NINE:
A Date with the Devil

"There's something you must remember...you are braver than you believe, stronger than you seem, and smarter than you think."

--Christopher Robin to Winnie the Pooh

I left my chemo consultation with a chemo schedule but I still had some trepidation. My sister Teressa thought it would be a good idea for me to talk to our family friend, Delaine. Delaine, my sisters, and I called ourselves cousins because we, along with her cousins and siblings, had all grown up attending my grandfather's church. Her grandparents were friends of my grandparents and her cousin, Yalonda, was one of my sister's best friends. Delaine had been diagnosed with colon cancer in her early thirties. By the time they'd discovered it she was already at stage IV. It had been a long time since I'd spoken to Delaine so I was unaware that she'd been going through chemotherapy off and on for four years. I didn't know anyone could go through chemo that long. I always thought they gave it a couple of tries and then sent you home to die if it didn't work. However, Delaine was being treated at MD Anderson in Houston and they do some pretty revolutionary clinical trials and treatments.

I was encouraged by Delaine's strength to endure all that she had for the last few years. There wasn't an end in sight for her like there was for me and she still had a positive attitude. It turned out that our chemo sessions were scheduled for the same days so we planned to talk to each other after treatments. I dubbed her my chemo buddy. She helped me settle in my mind that chemo was the best decision and that the side effects would be manageable. I figured if she could go through it for four years I could survive sixteen weeks.

I'd have my first chemo session the week of Thanksgiving. I was starting to feel secure in the fact that we had a plan of attack. Everything was going according to plan and then the unthinkable happened. I received my paycheck stub in the mail and it read that I'd been paid twenty-eight dollars and some change. *What the hell?!*

I'd seen people on the news who were in the throes of fighting a life threatening illness when their insurance denied them coverage or their jobs fired them so I was bracing myself for the unexpected and praying that nothing like that would happen to me. That's why I made sure to dot all of my i's and cross all of my t's prior to going on leave. I'd talked to my benefits person and did everything she told me to do. However, when I called her to complain about this puny check I received, she suddenly realized that I lived in California and employees in California follow different laws. I was supposed to apply for disability with the State and my job would make up the difference to ensure I received 60% of my salary. When I called the Employment Development Department (EDD) of California I was told that filing for State disability could take up to SIX WEEKS. I was livid!

Here we went again with my job screwing up. Luckily, Dr. Kendrick's receptionist had convinced me a few weeks earlier that I needed to apply for State disability just so that I could get all the money available to me while being off work. If she hadn't convinced me to apply I'd really have been in bad shape. Here I was preparing to go through chemo and I had to worry about how I was going to pay my bills. Not something that I needed to worry about while fighting for my life. Stress is the last thing you need when you're battling cancer but I seemed to have a lot of it. Thank God for parents! They loaned me the difference in pay and let me know to call on them if I needed anything at all. They wanted to make the experience as stress free as possible for me.

My parents were real gems as were my sisters. Each one of them came to town at different times. I have three sisters and we're all different shades of brown. My mom always jokes that each of us was darker and had nappier hair than the previous child. Funny but true. Teressa, the red bone of the family, flew in from Dallas to be with me during my first treatment. There were so many unknowns. *Would I be able to drive? Would I be bedridden? Or would I be one of the few patients who didn't experience very many side effects at all?* All we could do was wait and see.

Regardless of what the outcome would be my big sister wanted to be there for me. She came to town wearing the cutest wig. She has beautiful hair but likes the polished look wigs give her. She has the perfect face and head for them. Once I gave her a wig I bought in Paris for when I had bad hair days or couldn't find a stylist. It was a cute, short wig but I'd thought it didn't look that cute on me so I'd given it to her. When she put it on, it looked a lot sassier on her. I remember going to Dallas to visit her and she'd had it on when she picked me up. I said, "I like that wig!" To which she replied, "It's the one you gave me." I hadn't even recognized it. Some people just got "it."

Wigs aren't the only things Teressa brought with her. She came bearing gifts—gifts from her co-workers, some of whom I'd never met. As soon as we got to my apartment Teressa opened her luggage and pulled out presents for me. I got a pin of an angel holding a pink ribbon that also doubled as a Christmas ornament. I also received a Willow Tree angel figurine. The one I received is named Courage. She has her arms raised in triumph. I'm so inspired by her.

The last thing she pulled out was a prayer shawl and it was one of the most precious gifts I received. A lady at Teressa's job is part of a prayer shawl ministry at her church. The ladies in the ministry get together to crochet shawls and pray. They donate every prayer shawl they make to someone who is facing a tough time, for instance, recovering from an illness or the loss of a loved one. Each and every shawl is prayed over and they send this note with every one:

> "My Sister, My Brother, I have been praying to the Lord on your behalf. This shawl is filled with my prayers.
>
> During the good times, may it help you to feel the warmth and comfort that may be found in God's loving embrace. In times of trouble, may it help you to trust in the Lord and not be afraid.
>
> Whenever you wear it, may your soul find peace in the Lord.
>
> --The Shawl Maker"

My prayer shawl was beautiful. It was made with a variegated yarn of brown, purple, teal, and magenta and had a shimmery brown fringe on the ends. I absolutely loved it! Prayer is the most invaluable thing you can receive when you are battling a life threatening illness or any challenge in your life. When I wrapped myself in my shawl, it was a reminder that I was covered in prayer and wrapped in God's love.

The outpouring of love that I received was amazing to me. It was so encouraging. I was particularly moved by the reaction of my mom's older sister, Aunt Mary, who has a pretty tough exterior. I'd never seen her sensitive side but she called me in tears to tell me she was praying for me. She even sent me a gift and sent cards of encouragement regularly. The pastor of my church in Seattle and his wife, Pastor and Sis. Thornton, also sent me cards regularly and tucked a little money inside as well. Since I was a little girl I'd always been dear to Sis. Thornton's heart. She and her husband were close friends of my parents and her husband had been under my grandfather's tutelage when he was alive. My Aunt Suzie, who isn't really my aunt but just a close friend of my mom's, sent me cards and gifts regularly too. Diane, who referred me to Dr. Ferman, baked me gingerbread cookies since ginger is known to help with nausea. I received so many flowers, gifts, cards, phone calls, prayers, and well wishes. It really made a bitter time sweet.

As soon as Teressa got settled in I asked her if she wanted to see my breast. It was probably scary for some people to see but I knew it was still something they *wanted* to see. She said yes so we went in the bedroom where there was a mirror and I showed her my mastectomy scar. She handled seeing it very well. She wasn't freaked out by it in the least but she did say, "Oh sister! You are so brave. I couldn't lose my breasts." Teressa has big boobs. Her boobs are her best asset and her husband loves them. I'm sure for someone who really had an attachment to their breasts losing them could really be devastating but that wasn't the case for me.

"Yes, you could sister."

"No, I couldn't. I don't know what I'd do if I had to have my breasts removed."

"Well hopefully you never have to. Make sure to keep having your mammograms."

"I will. For sure."

It was nice that Teressa came to town when she did because I had a genetic testing appointment scheduled. They recommend that you bring a family member to listen to the information and help with details that you might have forgotten. My therapist took my blood and asked me a lot of questions with regard to my family's medical history as it pertained to cancer. She said cancer can be environmental, familial, or genetic. In my case, I didn't have either of the breast cancer gene mutations (BRCA1 or BRCA2) so my cancer was not classified as genetic. And since my grandmother had breast cancer after menopause, they didn't consider it familial. They figure if you live long enough you'll eventually get cancer so my grandmother having breast cancer in her eighties didn't signal to them that my cancer was familial. If my father had had a sister who'd also had breast cancer, then, because of there being a pattern, they would have considered it familial. Usually when breast cancer is inherited it'll affect the heiress, if you will, at a much younger age and will be more aggressive than the person you inherited it from. My having breast cancer so young makes me think it was inherited but we can't say since my dad doesn't have a sister. For that reason, my grandmother having cancer is considered to be a coincidence.

I strongly believe that my breast cancer is hereditary because my grandmother had breast cancer and her brother had prostate cancer, which is tied to the two known breast cancer genes. I don't have those particular genes but I think there are other similar genes that they aren't aware of yet. My grandmother could have had colon cancer or liver cancer or any other cancer but she had breast cancer and so did I. The genetic testing clinic kept my blood on file. In the event that they discover more breast cancer genes they can test my blood again. I think they will make some new discoveries in the future. Until they discover otherwise, my cancer was due to the environment—it could be carcinogens, pollutants, or just random.

I do have risk factors though according to the Gail Model. The Gail Model was named after Dr. Mitchell Gail of the National Cancer Institute and it uses a woman's medical and family history to determine her risk of developing invasive breast cancer. I menstruated young (around the age of nine or ten) and I never gave birth to a child. Another risk factor is that I was on birth control for several years. I can no longer use birth control with hormones since my cancer was estrogen and progesterone fed. Even given all of those risk factors, we're still not sure why I got breast cancer. The genetic counselor said that my cells had a one in over a million some odd chance of mutating and I was the "lucky" one. I try to think about how" lucky" I am when I play the lottery. My life suddenly changed for the worse one day when the odds were against me and it could suddenly change for the better with the odds against me.

The day Teressa and I went to chemo I was prepared with snacks and plenty of fluids so that I could flush those toxins out of my system as soon as possible. Everyone having infusions was over the hill and looked like death warmed over. I, on the other hand, was the youngest patient in the room. I had on some comfy sweats and my face was made up. I'm a believer that just because you're sick doesn't mean you have to look like it.

I picked out my reclining chair and got settled in. This day would be my first date with the devil. The Red Devil to be exact. That was the moniker given to Adriamycin, a very strong chemotherapy drug. In preparation for this hot date (pun intended), the nurse got all suited and booted in her protective suit, gloves, and eye shield. That's how powerful it is. They suit up to administer the drug but shoot it up my veins unreservedly. My nurse hung the red drip bag from my IV pole, connected me through my port and I just laid back and passed the time talking with my sister and reading fashion magazines. I was hooked up to an IV for four to five hours. Having someone there sure helped the time pass.

Because we weren't sure what to expect after the infusion I didn't make any plans to take Teressa sightseeing as I usually would for an out of town guest. We did, however, go shopping (my sister's favorite sport) the day after chemo. To my surprise I felt pretty good.

Teressa had flown all that way to take care of me and my first chemo session was uneventful. I felt a little guilty but at the same time I was thinking *If this is how it's going to be, this will be a piece of cake.*

The second chemo session was scheduled on a Thursday afternoon and that following Friday night was a rough one. Jamal said he was going down to the restaurant/lounge that was practically connected to our apartment complex to, as he said, "let his hair down." I was going to enjoy some "me time" and rest. And rest I did, that is until it started to get late and I was wondering where my husband was. Way past midnight Jamal finally came home and he was drunk out of his mind. He stormed into the apartment upset about an argument he'd had at the lounge. I couldn't make sense of what had gone on but I tried to calm him down and make sure he didn't stumble around our little apartment and break anything. He was like a bull in a china closet. I was up all night taking care of him when he should have been taking care of me. I was pissed that he would do this to me while I was fighting for my life. This was telling to me. Who does that to someone going through chemo? Needless to say, I got very little sleep.

What made it worse is the second treatment was not as easy as the first. With the first treatment, I guess enough of the drug hadn't built up in my system. The day of the chemo treatment was always fine. It was the subsequent days when the nausea set in that were hard. They gave me drugs to combat the queasies. However, my medicine bottle said to "take as needed," which conflicted with my paperwork from my doctor that said to take it "every twelve hours, round the clock." Not liking to take drugs, I tried to do with the least amount of medicine as possible. I wanted to take it as needed but I didn't know when I needed it. I didn't even realize what I was experiencing was nausea. I just felt icky, not really nauseated. Something I'd never really experienced before.

The day after I'd been up most of the night with Jamal, I don't know if I was too tired or what but I literally felt gross, like I was full of toxins. I felt so gross and miserable that I wanted to give up. I called my mom bawling, "Mom, I feel so horrible. I don't want to do this anymore. I'm ready to give up! If it's going to get worse, then I'm not going to be up for it." My mom, the woman of faith that she is, quickly replied, "We need to pray! You're gonna be okay baby. Let me call your sisters so we can all pray for you." Jamal was in the living room getting over his hangover and watching TV oblivious to what was going on with me. I sat up on the edge of the bed with tears streaming down my face as my mom got all of my sisters on the phone. They prayed for me one by one and encouraged me, telling me that I could get through it. They were my cheerleaders and prayer warriors. By the time I got off the phone with them I was a new person. It was like I had had an anxiety attack that their prayers had just made vanish. I felt a thousand times better. Prayer had never affected me so quickly the way their prayers did. Sometimes when you're weak you need other people's strength to draw on. It meant the world to me that they prayed me through my moment of weakness.

As for Jamal, he was so stressed out about going to jail, possibly losing his job, his embezzlement court case, and me having cancer. He didn't know how to deal with his feelings other than the way he had always dealt with them—drinking and bottling things up. I can't claim to know what it's like to see your loved one go through this—someone you love who was once full of life now lying in bed a lot, not eating, being hooked up to IV's, in pain, bald. I approached it so courageously that I expected everyone else to as well but I wasn't on the outside looking in.

One of my friends told me that her husband actually cheated on her while she was going through chemo. She later divorced him. I'd definitely put him in the dog category but who knows why men do the things that they do? Having had my own experience with my husband (not cheating but internalizing his emotions), I'd say that some men find cancer really difficult to deal with and instead of sacrificing their feelings for a while and putting themselves in their wife or partner's shoes, they're more concerned with their feelings, what they aren't getting, how the normality of their life is changing, and how they might lose their loved one. Instead of the thought of losing their wife or partner inspiring them to make the challenging times as comfortable as possible for her, they start feeling sorry for themselves and get swallowed up by their emotions. Then there are other men who go into caregiver mode and deal with the stress just fine. Everybody's different and you never know how someone is going to deal with stress until they're faced with it. Cancer will definitely separate the boys from the men.

Jamal really took it hard when he needed to shave my head. My hair came out exactly when Dr. Scott said it would. It was about a week after my second treatment and my scalp got really tender to the touch. If I scratched my head I could feel my hair detach from the scalp. I'd noticed that it was shedding a lot and told Jamal that I needed to shave it but he along with several of my family members were hoping that I'd be part of the roughly 8% of patients who don't lose their hair.

It was Christmas Eve when I'd had enough. Treating my hair with kid gloves was getting on my nerves. I wanted my hair off of my head. Jamal had agreed to shave it for me when the time came, but when I told him I was ready, he insisted that I was making my hair come out by playing in it and he told me to wait. This time I wasn't taking no for an answer.

"Honey, my hair is coming out. I think it's time for you to shave it."

"If you would stop playing in it, it wouldn't be coming out. Leave it alone," he replied.

"What? Do you want me to not comb it? Just leave it like this for days?" I had it in an up-do. I suppose he wanted me to just put a scarf on at night and wake up flawless but that's not how it works. I'd need to put a brush or comb to it. "It's not me that's making it come out. I'm losing my hair and I don't want to see huge patches coming out," I said.

"Well, go in the bathroom and get yourself mentally prepared," he said, with a nervous look on his face. I could tell that he really hadn't wanted this day to come. He'd always liked me with longer hair to the point that, when I had shorter hair and he saw a picture of me with longer hair he said, "That's the Karla I know." As if my hair made me who I am.

"I *am* mentally prepared," I said. "I think *you* need to get mentally prepared. I just want to get this done. Tomorrow I can wear my wig over to your parents' house, and your mom and Toni can let me know how I look." I didn't have anyone to try my looks out on except Jamal. This was new for me since I usually had my mom and three sisters to act as my fashion police.

I went into the bathroom, got the clippers out and waited for Jamal to get up the courage to shave my head. He came into the bathroom, turned on the clippers, and when he ran them across my scalp most of my hair just fell out without much prodding. He could tell that what I was saying was true. My hair was hanging on by a thread. I knew seeing me without hair would make all of this real to him. I made sure to have on makeup and earrings so I wouldn't look too bad. Not just for him but for myself too.

I actually didn't look that bad. You never know what your head might look like without your hair. I took pictures of my new look. I even took one with Jamal who shaved his head normally anyway. His facial expression said it all. I was smiling so he tried to smile with me but you could still see the sadness in his face. The two of us with our bald heads (he voluntarily, me involuntarily) looked like Mr. and Mrs. Clean.

I emailed the pictures to my family since they weren't in California with me. They wanted to know everything that I was going through. My sister, Michelle, happened to be at my parents' house when she got my email. I was on the phone with her as she looked at the pictures. I said, "What do you think? I don't think I look that bad. I still look healthy." She said crying,

"You look beautiful! You don't look sick at all. That makes me feel better." My dad came into the room and asked what she was looking at. She said, "Karla just shaved her head. Do you want to see?" He told her he couldn't look at me without hair or he might cry. My dad isn't a crier, but like most men he thinks a woman's hair is her crown and glory. And like most people, he associates cancer with hair loss, so seeing me bald would just drive it home that I had cancer. Michelle said, "Come on dad. You can look. It's not that bad. She doesn't look sick." He finally acquiesced and managed not to shed a tear. He even said that I looked pretty.

Jamal thought I looked pretty too but for some reason, the day he shaved my head was the beginning of the end of our sex life. I thought for sure when I lost my breast that sex might slow down but it didn't. It was the hair loss along with the chemo side effects that made Jamal think I was delicate—too delicate to have sex with. Dr. Scott told me that I might have a low libido and might experience some vaginal dryness but none of that happened. My sex drive was normal and I wanted to be made love to, but Jamal had too much on his mind and never was in the mood. He told me that, when a man saw his wife going through the experience of cancer treatment, sex was the last thing on his mind. I, on the other hand, was thinking: *What if I die tomorrow? I don't want to die not having had enough sex.* I don't know if there's sex in heaven. I know Muslims believe their martyrs will go to heaven and have forty virgins. However, I don't think when I die there will be forty hot, sexy men at my disposal. This is it. I would think Jamal would try to give me everything I could ask for right now. Even a prisoner on death row gets a last meal.

How did I feel about losing my hair? I wasn't that distraught about it. I'd cut it off a few years prior and wore it short and natural because I was tired of being a slave to relaxers a.k.a the creamy crack. I wondered what it was that I was running to cover up every six weeks when I got a touch-up and I was tired of going to the hair salon and coming out not feeling like I'd gotten my money's worth. As a matter of fact, when I arrived in Paris to live, I had natural hair and only relaxed it once I figured I couldn't find someone to cut it like I wanted.

Given our hair history and the versatility of our hair, I think black women may feel less anxiety about losing their hair than other races of women. Most of us have worn wigs, weaves, braids, etc. We mostly see hair as an accessory. The only sad thing for me about losing my hair was that I was growing it out and it was finally getting long when it all fell out. But I knew it would grow back. If it didn't, which would be highly unlikely, I'd invest in a nice lace front wig and keep it moving.

My doctor gave me a prescription for a cranial prosthesis, the clinical term for wig, and referred me to a few wig distributors, but I wound up going to black beauty supply stores or ordering wigs online that were a fraction of the cost and way more stylish. When I went to those wig shops my doctor referred me to I thought *Wow! White women don't know that they can get a cute wig for less than $300. You can get several wigs for that price.*

And I had several wigs—a short, spikey, auburn wig; a short black, cropped wig; a long, layered, brunette wig with auburn highlights; a long, black wig with a flip; a long black wig that looked flat ironed. It was great! But there was one little problem: I was paranoid that sometimes I looked like a cancer patient. For me, it was one thing to be healthy and wear a wig, and a totally different thing to have cancer and wear a wig when you're bald. We've all seen those people wearing wigs who you can just tell are sick. I didn't want to look like that. The minute

someone looked at my wig, which they could have been looking at because it was cute, I thought it was because it was obvious that I had a wig on. I rarely wore sunglasses when I had on
a wig because I felt like I was in the witness protection program,
or I thought people might think I was going to "set it off" like
in the movie by the same name starring Queen Latifah. Not a
good look.

Although a lot of people wanted to see me bald, I never
went out of the house without some hair on my head. I think
people who know you are battling cancer want to see you with
a bald head for some reason. I don't know what it does for them
but I let all of my friends and family know that they wouldn't see
me out of the house without a wig. My younger sister, Brianna,
even offered to shave her head in solidarity with me. I told her
not to bother because no one was ever going to see my bald
head. There are some people who have the style and grace to
wear a bald head. I didn't dress the part. I had the grace but
not the style. I would have looked like someone who needed
some hair. I couldn't have pulled it off unless I had a wardrobe
change. I much preferred to add to my wardrobe with wigs than
to change my dressing style all together. Therefore, I bought
wigs and had fun changing up my look.

There were others who wanted me to wear a scarf and some
big sunglasses because I have the face to carry it off, but how
many people do you see going around with a scarf and sunglasses on? Usually people who do that and look stylish have
hair and you can tell the difference between a scarf on a bald
head and a scarf on a head full of hair. Besides, wearing a scarf
on your head wasn't *a la mode* and it just wasn't me. I didn't
want the attention or the pity. I wanted to look as normal as
possible. Confidence is the rule of thumb with any look. If you
aren't confident you can't pull it off.

Looking normal became harder and harder the more treatments I had. My tongue had brown spots on it and the palms of my hands and feet darkened. You could no longer see where my palms started or ended. I looked like I'd been working on cars and needed some Goop. My grease monkey uncle always used Goop to clean his hands when they were black with oil stains.

I stopped getting manicures or pedicures until my palms turned back to normal. That was a mistake. I could have explained what I was going through. I thought the manicurists would think I had a communicable disease. I didn't want to draw attention to myself or have them talking about me in Korean or Vietnamese so I stayed away.

Another side effect was that my eyes would tear up for no reason. At times it looked like I was crying. It would just drip and drip out of nowhere. Put all those side effects together and I felt like I looked a hot ass mess at times. I usually looked and felt better the further out I got from treatment. I was still pretty cute for a cancer patient. I had my hang ups but at first glance I looked healthy.

Those were my visual side effects but the ones no one could see were the worst. I had a full medicine chest because of chemo and surgery. You name the condition, I had something to relieve it. My bowels were literally a pain in my ass. I had every kind of laxative you could get on the market trying to find the right one. From the time I had my mastectomy, I was buying laxatives. First of all, the dummies at the hospital let me go without having a bowel movement. I didn't realize how much of a problem that would pose—four days and no BM. The nurse told me to buy a laxative when I left but she didn't tell me how much pain I'd be in trying to have a movement. It was worse than having a baby I'm sure. At least when you have a baby you dilate. I wanted to kill the nurses and doctors at the hospital.

The narcotics were to blame and to this day I won't take them. Even for the excruciating migraine headaches caused by the chemo that hurt so bad they made me scream I wouldn't take narcotics. No way, no how. I only take over the counter or prescription strength Ibuprofen. My bum thanks me.

My bowels went from one extreme to the next. I swear by Immodium when you need to firm things up. I never travel near or far without it. Women are notorious for carrying around pain killers for headaches and cramps. My point of view is that you can ask someone for pain killers but if you get diarrhea, who has something to help you? No one, usually, which means a trip to the drug store. Anything could happen on the way. I don't get diarrhea often but I like to be prepared if the time comes.

There was one side effect that wasn't a result of any medication. I've always been someone who would imagine my life down the road—make goals and see what those goals would look like in my mind's eye. But I realized once treatment started that, no matter how hard I tried, I couldn't visualize the future. My mind's eye became very nearsighted. I think fear had hindered my vision. I literally had to take things one day at a time because I couldn't see myself one year out let alone five years out.

I finished my first four rounds of the Red Devil with flying colors. No major side effects or reactions. By the time I got to the fourth session I'd figured out how to take my nausea medicine properly which meant round the clock but I wouldn't need it for my next four rounds. Everyone said the next drug would be a lot easier than the Red Devil. It would be marked by pain, which was apparently more manageable than the nausea. With my medicine chest I was ready for anything.

Karla's Column

Karla after Her Mastectomy, before Her Hair Fell Out |
Dublin, CA

Karla Just after Jamal Shaved Her Head | Dublin, CA

Karla in Three of Her Wigs | Dublin, CA

CHAPTER TEN:
Making Sense of Religion

"Into each life some rain must fall."

--Henry Wadsworth Longfellow

I was so mad at God during the time leading up to my cancer diagnosis. I felt like I had done everything right but wasn't getting anything but struggle in return. Once I got the diagnosis, all of those frustrations organically moved to the back burner. Cancer was serious and I needed God to get through this. I still wanted some answers though. As if I wasn't struggling enough He saw fit to pile on cancer? Knowing that I'd have a lot of time on my hands, I was looking forward to getting quiet, clearing my mind, and making sense of my relationship with the Almighty.

My frustration with Him started when I came home from Paris and started looking for a job. I was at my wit's end. Why was it taking so long for me to find a job? I religiously paid my tithes and gave my offerings, so I was expecting the windows of heaven to pour me out a blessing that I didn't have room enough to receive like pastors always preached just before taking an offering. Instead, I was broke and out of work for an entire year. When I was finally hired, my pay was all screwed up and I kept having all kinds of financial setbacks. I'd had it up to my ears with faith and then I was diagnosed with cancer and that really made me ask myself *What's it all for? What is life all about? Was I learning who God is for myself or was I expecting Him to be what everyone told me to expect Him to be?* I needed some answers.

What baffled me about the cancer diagnosis was that I hadn't seen it coming. Although I wasn't thrilled with God at the time of my diagnosis, I thought we had an understanding. God always spoke to me through dreams. Every miscarriage that I'd had was foreshadowed in a dream that at first seemed evil to me but I later found to be God's way of bracing me for what was about to happen. At the time, my marriage wasn't where I felt it needed to be in order for us to have kids but Jamal insisted that it was. I wasn't going to be one of those women who snuck birth control pills behind her husband's back like I'd seen in soap operas. I wanted to be a good wife so I asked God not to give me any kids until my marriage was solid. I got pregnant four times but I never got out of the first trimester. One time I didn't have a period for a while and thought something was wrong with me. A pregnancy test revealed that I wasn't pregnant so my doctor recommended that I have an ultrasound. It turned out that I had a cyst in my uterus that my doctor said was sitting right by my cervix acting like an IUD. This experience let me know that regardless of how much of an accident we think kids are, there are no accidents when a child is carried to term. It's a miracle to have a child and I look at it as a miracle that I didn't have any kids. It was by design. I always thought when the time was right I'd probably have no problem having kids.

When I was separated from Jamal, I decided that I wouldn't divorce him until I knew God told me it was okay. I had a dream after three years of separation that let me know clearly that I was to divorce Jamal. In my dream Jamal called me to ask what I wanted to do about our marriage. I wanted to make it work but I'd grown weary of making all of the effort. I told him that I wasn't going to beg him anymore. That's when Jamal said, "Let's just *forfeit* this."

When I awoke from the dream I had to look up the word forfeit. I'd only heard it in reference to sports. I didn't know it had any other meaning.

One definition of forfeit is that it's to lose something due to neglect of duty or breach of contract. At the time, I was living in Seattle and Jamal was living in California. I totally felt like Jamal had neglected his duty as a husband and therefore had breached our marriage contract. Every time I spoke to him I'd ask what he wanted to do about our marriage (would he move back to Seattle or would I move to California?), and he always changed the subject. I had no idea what he was doing in California, but I knew that God did and He obviously thought divorcing Jamal was okay.

Boy, that threw some religious people at my church for a loop. After getting an understanding of that dream, I didn't have any reservations about divorcing Jamal because I knew I'd heard from God. Other people who put God in a box and were told that God hates divorce and believed that God would fix every marriage couldn't make sense of me believing that God had told me to divorce my husband. Divorce wasn't of God. It was of the Devil. But to the contrary, there are allowable reasons for divorce and abandonment is one of them. The only thing that confused me about my permission to divorce Jamal was that I'd really believed in my heart, prior to the dream, that God had inspired me to give an offering to Jamal's church in California in faith that my marriage would be restored. I was confused and needed to hear from God as to why I was getting conflicting messages. That's when God let me know that I'd divorce Jamal and then remarry him.

I was always told that when you think you're hearing from God to get confirmation from the Bible. God and His Word shouldn't conflict. When I told God that He had to show me where someone in the Bible had divorced and remarried the same person, He led me to Jeremiah 31:31-32. In those passages God is speaking to the children of Israel and He tells them that He would make a new and better covenant with them because He was a husband to their forefathers but that they broke His covenant. Basically, God married the children of Israel, divorced them, and married them again. That's what would happen with me and Jamal.

I really believed it to be true but I didn't harp on it. In fact, as time passed, I was looking forward to something new and had moved on with my life. But it makes sense that God would answer my prayer to restore my marriage even if it would be almost ten years later. I'd cried and prayed myself to sleep so many nights when I was first separated that He was probably sick of me. Reminds me of the story in the Bible where Jesus says that a judge finally acquiesced to a widow's plea because she was so persistent and just kept asking.

Another experience I had with God is when He healed me of hypothyroidism. My hypothyroidism was making my life miserable. I was a total mess. I would wake up in the morning and just stare at the ceiling wishing that I could move but I couldn't or wouldn't. My eyes were puffy, my hair was brittle and my skin was dry. I was physically exhausted and I was severely depressed. I was at an all-time low. It didn't help that this was the time I was going through my separation and miscarriages.

I'd been to my endocrinologist and every time I paid a visit they took my blood and he would adjust my Synthroid dosage. I was feeling like shit and whatever he did wasn't working. My doctor told me that once you have hypothyroidism you're stuck with it for life but I decided to believe what I'd been hearing on Christian television and reading in the Bible. God was still in the healing business. I just needed to have faith.

During my separation I decided to go all out for God. Before that I was a believer but wasn't really going to church or reading the Bible on a regular basis. This time I wanted to get what the Bible promised to me. I listened to every sermon on healing. I had the healing scriptures on tape. I read those scriptures where Jesus healed people over and over again until I really believed that God would do it for me. One day I woke up and started to take my thyroid medicine and I just couldn't put it in my mouth. I'd started to feel like I was at a toxic level. When I looked at the pill I felt like it was something that was poisoning me so I stopped taking it. The next time I went to the doctor I told him what had happened and he said that he didn't advise stopping thyroid medicine cold turkey but when he took my blood sample I was fine and I've continued to be fine ever since. Hypothyroidism was one thing but cancer was a whole other thing. I'd need super-sized faith to be healed of this.

I was thrown for a loop with this cancer diagnosis. God didn't prepare me for this. Something this serious should have been revealed in a dream. I didn't have a dream that stuck out in my mind as being prophetic. Maybe that meant my having cancer wasn't anything serious. Just a bump in the road. Maybe God didn't forewarn me because I'd handle it just fine. Or maybe He did forewarn me and I just didn't get it.

There was this one experience that I'd had several years

before I got cancer. One October, almost a year before my grandmother was diagnosed with breast cancer, I was helping a friend drive from Seattle to Denver. She was relocating to be closer to her boyfriend. I let her know that there was one thing I needed to do if I was going to Denver and that was visit the art museum. I love art and I think you can learn a lot about what's important to a city by what they have in their museums. Any city that I visit I try to stop by the museum. The Denver Art Museum (DAM) has some beautiful American art. I'd never appreciated American artists until visiting that museum. It also has a really nice collection of Native American art and artifacts. I remember going through the Native American section and seeing a Native American man viewing the collection. I was almost moved to tears to see a man from a race that had almost been wiped out viewing artifacts of his heritage. It was hard to believe that American Indians were once the majority in this country and now you hardly see them. It was also interesting to learn how many of the states and cities have Indian names or are named after American Indian chiefs.

My visit to the DAM was both educational and moving. When my friend, her boyfriend, and I left, we drove down a side street of the museum. I remember the trees lining the street were full of colorful leaves. Pink ribbons adorned their branches and were waving in the autumn breeze. It was like they were waving in slow motion in order for me to pay attention and I thought to myself *Someone close to me is going to get breast cancer.* I knew I needed to brace myself for the bad news. Several months later I heard that my grandmother had breast cancer. For some reason I never really felt the vision of pink ribbons was about her. But no one else got breast cancer so I thought it must be her. However, she was in her eighties when she was diagnosed. Although I was very sad about her diagnosis I consider myself to be a pragmatist. You have to die of something and she had lived a good life. The message in the vision felt monumental. The scale of it seemed like pink ribbons, or more specifically what pink ribbons represent, would be a major part of my life. Thinking back on it, maybe it was for me. Maybe God wasn't being silent.

Even with the pink ribbon vision there's still the question of why I got cancer. My sister, Michelle, is the one who experimented with smoking in her twenties and has a fast food diet. I swear every time I call that girl she is going through a drive-thru. That can't be good for you but she didn't get cancer. I did.

Why am I the cesspool of my parents' genes? I'm the one who had asthma, allergies, eczema, hypothyroidism, stretch marks, miscarriages (although I prayed not to have kids), lop-sided, saggy breasts, yaws, and now cancer, not my sisters. In case you're wondering what yaws is, it's a rare skin rash that's supposed to be common in third world countries not North America. Don't ask me how I got it. When my sisters got wind of the news that I had yaws, they teased me. They'd sneak up on me and say, "Yaw!" or call me "Yaw bitch." It was slightly cruel but, depending on what mood I was in, it was pretty funny.

Over the thirty four years that I'd lived, I tried to be a good person and I felt like I had so much more to offer the world than what had come to fruition thus far in my life. I've always wondered if people die before they've fulfilled their purpose. When I was diagnosed I thought *If this is it, I'll know the answer because I have so much more to offer the world.*

God didn't speak to me about why I got cancer but there's a Bible verse that I've always liked. It says that God sends the rain on the just and the unjust alike. Basically, shit happens regardless of whether or not we consider ourselves to be good in the eyes of God. Yes, I just cussed after talking about a Bible verse but

I'm just keeping it real. Religion can mess you up and for years "The Church" or Bible believers would have had me believe that only Christians have the answers. However, things happen every day that are contrary to what "The Church" would have you believe. Christians do get sick and Christians die every day, several times a day. So do Buddhists, Atheists, Catholics, and all other kinds of religious people. There is no religious shield that Christians get once they profess Christ that isn't available to non-believers but protects Christians from diseases. They would have you think so but it's not true. Shit happens and it happens to those who are good and those who are bad.

There's a lot in life we can't explain. Like why do cantankerous people live so long but the good die young? Why are women who would make great mothers barren while crack addicts and unwed teens have no problem having babies? Why do people have class and no money while others have money and no class? Why do rednecks always win the lottery? Who knows?! But one thing I do know is that there's a God and He's still in the healing business and He's still making and keeping His promises. Will He heal me of cancer? I don't know. I suppose if it suits His purposes, He will. Likewise, if it suits His purposes, He won't. Can He heal me of cancer? Absolutely! Is anything too hard for God?

I decided to take God out of the box I had Him in and to stop trying to anticipate His next move in my life. No more letting people tell me who God is, what He's supposed to do for me, or His likes and dislikes. I'd just live and learn for myself. I let all of my frustrations go and focused on being grateful and optimistic.

CHAPTER ELEVEN:
A New Year, a New Outlook

"If you're going through hell, keep going."

--Winston Churchill

Karla's Column

On 1/2/08 3:10 PM, "Karla" <karla@email.com> wrote:

Dear Ms. Richardson,

I am finally getting around to thanking you for sending me the September 2007 issue of *Vogue*. I'm not sure if my mother told you but the receptionist at my breast surgeon's office gave me her issue to keep me busy while I recovered from my mastectomy. My mother just had to look through it and wound up leaving it at a restaurant about forty five minutes away (at least, that's the last time we remember having it). I was so disappointed because I knew it wasn't on shelves any longer.

My mom vowed to get another copy but she's not the most computer savvy so I wasn't really expecting her to get in contact with the right people. Needless to say, I was so impressed when she forwarded me your email.

The magazine arrived the day before my surgery and I was so excited—absolutely perfect timing. After living in Paris for a year and a half and returning to the States in May of 2006, the magazine is my little escape to Paris, the land of luxury. That issue now has special meaning to me. Not to mention I love to tell people that someone at *Vogue* personally sent me a hard to find issue of the magazine as an act of kindness.

Battling breast cancer has been challenging but so many people that I know and some that I've never met have been so kind and thoughtful that it truly has made a bitter situation sweet. I just wanted to make sure that you know that your kindness was appreciated.

Best wishes for a prosperous new year!

Karla Mitchell

From: Vogue (email@vogue.com)

Sent: Wed January 2, 2008, 1:34 pm

To: Karla (karla@email.com)

Dear Ms. Mitchell,

How kind of you—in the midst of what must be a difficult time for you—to send a note about my sending you the September issue of *Vogue!* You are very welcome to it. I'm very glad it was something that you enjoyed after your operation. And I do hope that you will have a successful recovery and a very happy New Year!

Ms. Richardson

Vogue Information

Email to my cousin in St. Vincent, West Indies

From: Karla (karla@email.com)

Sent: On Jan 10, 2008, at 1:37 PM,

To: Rosalind (rosalind@email.com)

Karla wrote:

Hi Roz. Thank you for the prayers, well wishes, and beautiful card. It was very sweet. I love the message in it.

I'm doing well. I'm looking forward to being

cured this year. The year will be half over by the time I'm done with everything but I'm trying to look at it as the year that I will be healthy. Today is the halfway mark for my chemo. I have my last treatment of one drug today and start another one in two weeks. The next drug will not cause nausea so I'm looking forward to that. The good news is that I look great. No one would know that I'm a cancer patient and I like to keep it that way. ;) I don't feel all that bad either except for the four to five days following chemo.

Well I'd better get ready for my treatment today. Keep me in your prayers. Have a fabulous New Year!!! Give my regards to everyone.

Love,

Karla

I started my Taxol treatment feeling like it was going to be smooth sailing. After all, I'd made it past the Red Devil. Taxol didn't have any fancy monikers so I figured it couldn't be all that bad.

Taxol was my halfway point—halfway through chemo. I'd started to feel like I had treatment down. I had a regular chemo partner, Jamal's sister, Toni. I liked having Toni drive me to chemo because she has a BMW 7 Series and I could ride to treatment in style instead of being in my little economy car. Toni also had a lot of good movies on DVD and she'd bring along an assortment of lottery scratch tickets. In fact, I credit her with getting me started scratching. I'd scratched lottery tickets before but not on a regular basis. Now that my excitement was at a minimum, I found it to be a good source of an adrenaline rush. It was filling a void for me I guess.

My other form of entertainment was politics. Not a likely source for me but given that George W. Bush was nearing the end of his last term and people were fed up with his style of governing, Democrats had a chance of winning the next election and thereby putting either the first woman or first African American in the White House. I'd been hearing a lot about Barack Obama, a freshman senator from Illinois of African and Caucasian descent who was running for president. He and Hillary Clinton were the forerunners in the democratic race. Both were running on the promise of reforming health care, which was an issue very close to home now. I'd be someone with a pre-existing condition and I didn't want medical coverage to be the deciding factor in whether or not I moved up in my career. If the laws didn't change I could be stuck at my job until I found another company with insurance that covered pre-existing conditions.

Like I said I wasn't really into politics but I did feel it was my duty to vote. Jamal had already decided that Barack Obama was getting his vote. I wasn't so sure. I didn't understand the primary process at the time. I'm pretty sure that in the past I just voted in the general election and ignored the primaries. This time, I was so fed up with Republicans that I wanted them out of office. My goal was to make sure someone who could beat the Republican candidate in the general election would be our nominee. In my mind, Hillary Clinton, was a shoo-in. Everyone knew her and loved her husband, Former President Bill Clinton. Surely she could win and surely she could beat the Republican candidate. I had my mind pretty set until Jamal told me that I was missing out on making history. Barack Obama, albeit virtually unknown to most of us aside from his speech at the 2004 Democratic National Convention, was well qualified, capable and quite possibly could be our first black president. It wasn't going to be a case like when Jesse Jackson or Al Sharpton ran for president and mostly gained the black vote. Even white people believed in and supported this man. That was all fine and well but I didn't want a repeat Bradley Effect. The Bradley Effect had come about when a black mayor had run for governor in California in 1982. In polls people had said they'd vote for him and he was pegged to win but he lost. The theory is that many white people said they'd vote for him but couldn't bring themselves to do it or perhaps they told the pollster they'd vote for him so they wouldn't look prejudiced. The last thing I wanted was for votes to be divided and as a result we put the wrong person up against a Republican candidate. And I didn't want people to support Barack Obama in the primary and then not enough people support him in the general election. My concern was *Is America ready for a black president?* More and more it became evident that it just might be. Prominent politicians and celebrities came out in support of Barack Obama daily.

The one that convinced me was Senator Ted Kennedy. I knew he was most likely good friends with the Clintons but there was something he saw in Barack Obama that made him endorse him. That along with Hillary Clinton being moved to tears during the campaign pushed me into Barack Obama's corner. Hillary is tough but I just don't think the president of the United States should be crying over a hard campaign. It was a sign of weakness to me and it lost my vote. However, it seemed to work for her in the polls—at least among women.

When I started my Taxol treatment the primaries were just

getting underway. There was still a lot of mudslinging and vetting going on, which added a little drama and suspense. But it was also a very exciting time because Barack Obama's race for the White House was more of a movement than a campaign. There was a palpable optimism and energy. Obama was someone new. He didn't come from privilege or a political lineage. He hadn't been in office long enough to become jaded, tainted, or complacent. He had a lot of great ideas and you could tell that he would TCB (take care of business). He wasn't a know-it-all and, although he was a freshman senator you knew that whatever he didn't know he'd learn by surrounding himself with great advisors. America was excited about Barack Obama and so was the world. If I had a nickel for every time someone told me how much they couldn't stand George Bush when I was in France, I'd have my student loans paid off. I was looking forward to having a president who could help repair our reputation as being self-centered bullies who thought we were better than everyone else. Once I cast my vote for Barack Obama in the primary election, I became an Obama for America supporter and volunteered from time to time.

Taxol was definitely different than the Red Devil but I wouldn't call it easier. Just like the Red Devil, my first treatment was fine but the second treatment tested my limits. That's when the excruciating bone pain kicked in. It felt like someone had put my legs in a vice grip. Couple that with the fact that I caught a cold during round two and I thought I was going to die. Seriously, I thought I was close. I was running a fever of one hundred four degrees. Since my fever wouldn't subside I had to make an emergency visit to see Dr. Scott. She was surprised to see me because they were just saying how I'd done so well on chemo—I hadn't had to come in for any bad reactions to the drugs. I guess she spoke too soon.

With what the drugs do to your white blood cell count during chemo you're more susceptible to getting infections and if you do get an infection it's a lot harder for you to fight it off. Dr. Scott took my blood to get my cell count, gave me a white cell booster, and told me to take some Tylenol for my fever. I was surprised to learn I just had a cold and not some sort of major virus.

There wasn't much Dr. Scott could do about the bone pain. I already had drugs at home. It was just a matter of me deciding what I wanted to take. I stuck with Ibuprofen for obvious reasons but popped a few extra. That offered a slight alleviation but nothing could totally rid me of this pain. Thankfully, once I got past the second treatment it let up a little. But while it let up, other side effects reared their ugly heads.

I was warned that I could have peripheral neuropathy which would feel kind of like when your foot falls asleep—"tingling" of the hands and feet. Oh how I wish it had only been a little tingling. Tingling must have been the mild case of peripheral neuropathy. What I had would then be classified as a severe case because it felt like thousands of little needle pricks on my feet or like someone had put itching powder in my shoes. Thank God I didn't have it in my hands! It's hard to describe but I saw a commercial that talked about neuropathy and it showed a swarm of bees stinging a person's feet. That, to me, most accurately depicts what it felt like. It was the worst because you never knew when it would hit. I'd be fine and then all of a sudden my feet started to itch relentlessly. I hated leaving the house because I was worried that my neuropathy would kick in.

My other irritating side effect was hot flashes, which I learned was just something I'd have to live with since I'd be taking Tamoxifen after radiation and that would also cause hot flashes. Here I was, thirty-four years old and I would have to live with hot flashes. Basically, I'd suffer through menopause twice. Once now and once later should the good Lord allow me to live long enough to reach the change of life naturally. I was not a happy camper. First of all, I sweat like a pig normally so the slightest bit of heat made me sweat bullets. Secondly, you might as well call the wig a hairy hat because when a hot flash hit that's what it felt like. There were many times I felt like ripping that thing off in public. It's very hard to look and feel good when you're wearing a wig while having a hot flash and sweat is dripping down your face. You can believe that when I was in the comfort of my home I didn't wear a wig, especially once the hot flashes hit. I also didn't bother with putting on foundation or powder. I just sweated it off anyway. Luckily, a smooth, even complexion is one good thing my parents passed my way.

Taxol also gave me an alter ego. I don't know if it was the steroids I had to receive before the Taxol infusion or what, but I'd get so hungry, to the point that I'd turn into the biggest bitch if I didn't eat something right away. When I say turn into the biggest bitch, I mean zero to bitch in three seconds. Since this happened often and was so out of character for me, Jamal and I gave my alter ego a name—Ferocia (pronounced Fuh-rOsh-a)—as in "ferocious," which described my appetite. If Ferocia paid a visit it meant that I'd better get some food ASAP or heads were gonna roll. One time she manifested on the forty five minute drive home from my in-laws' and we drove like mad to get me to Chili's, the nearest sit down restaurant. Ferocia was very particular. She didn't eat just anything. It had to be appetizing. She didn't want fast food but she did want food fast. We'd definitely need some bread or chips and salsa when my butt hit the booth seat. We got into the restaurant and headed straight for the bar because there's always faster service in the bar. I apologized in advance to the waitress and let her know that I was on medication that makes me very hungry and asked her to bring out some chips and salsa right away. Thankfully, she was very accommodating so nobody got hurt. After I ate the chips and nibbled on a few bites of my food I was full and Ferocia went away. Jamal was so frustrated that I would go through all of that hoopla to only eat a few bites but I truly was at the mercy of Ferocia and my appetite. It seemed like I'd be able to eat a horse but then once I had the food in front of me I could only eat a little. I learned to keep a granola bar or SlimFast handy to help keep Ferocia at bay.

When chemotherapy was almost over I was able to see Dr. Galani and have him add saline to the expander he'd placed in my breast during my mastectomy. The first time he added saline I could hardly turn my neck to look behind me while driving it was so tight. However, slowly but surely the muscle and skin started to give and it wasn't so bad. I felt like a pubescent little girl seeing my breast grow before my eyes, looking at it each time to see how much bigger it was getting and how it looked in my clothes. It was an exciting time but also very frustrating. The expanding breast is awkward. The shape of it isn't quite what a real breast would be like so it was a pain to try to get dressed. I still had the saggy right breast that wasn't going to be lifted until the reconstruction. So I had what felt like a small melon on my chest trying to match a saggy breast. You think you have clothes for it but trust me you don't. You'll probably have a couple of things that fit right but as soon as you get another expansion they may not work. I had some push up pads from when I'd had two good breasts that came in handy.

My younger sister, Brianna, and my parents came to town to celebrate my last treatment. I could only have one person with me at a time so they took turns sitting with me. I'd imagined I would have my last treatment and bring in cupcakes and make a big deal about it. But when the day came I didn't really do anything. I was just excited to be done with it all. Just having my family there was enough of a celebration for me.

My last treatment went off without a hitch and after resting for a couple of days I decided to take Brianna to San Francisco. Brianna is the baby of the family. I was the baby for about nine years because my parents thought they were finished having kids. And I'm sure they were until I got it in my mind that I wanted a baby sister or brother (sibling wasn't in my vocabulary then). This was around the same time that I was asking God for breasts. If I remember correctly I think I'd recently been baptized so maybe I thought I could just ask God for all kinds of things. I was tired of being the younger sister and being left out. Sometimes my sisters would complain about having to take me places or say I was too young to join them. I decided that I wanted to be a big sister and I would never treat my little sister how they treated me. So at night when my parents were in bed, I'd knock on their door and ask them if they were making my little brother or sister. I did this quite frequently until one day my mother was pregnant and I got my baby sister. I've tried to be the best big sister to her. Brianna has a gift for music just like my mom and I'd sit at the kitchen table with her when she practiced her flute. I was at every one of her recitals. I have her and Looney Tunes to thank for my appreciation of classical music.

(As an adult I realized how much classical music I was exposed to by watching Bugs Bunny.)

Brianna loves to travel but had never been to the Bay Area before. I didn't want her to come all that way and just see my tiny apartment. We rode BART (Bay Area Rapid Transit) to Embarcadero and walked around Fisherman's Wharf. We were strolling along, looking around one of the souvenir shops when all of a sudden my feet started to itch like crazy.

"Ugh! I was hoping this wouldn't happen!"

"What's wrong sister?"

"My feet are starting to itch!" I said as I stomped my feet on the floor. Stomping my feet on the floor really only helped for the split second when my sole made contact with the ground but it was the only consolation I had. I had never been on an outing when my neuropathy hit. I pretty much stayed at home to avoid a situation like this where I had to try to look normal when all I really wanted to do is scream and rip my socks and shoes off and scratch my feet incessantly. I tried to grin and bear it but nothing doing. We quickly called an end to our sightseeing but were at least able to take a trolley to the Powell Street BART station so that Bri could see Lombard Street and some other views of the city. It was the quickest way back anyway since we would have had quite a trek to get back to the Embarcadero BART station.

I'd had enough of my "tingling" feet and called Dr. Scott to let her know that something needed to be done. I'd mentioned it to my nurse practitioner before but she told me that it would get better, but it didn't. I don't think they realized that it was worse than tingling so perhaps that's why they didn't take it more seriously until I put my foot down (no pun intended). Once they understood that it was unbearable they prescribed me a drug that actually made it go away. I was thrilled but I gained five pounds right away once I started the medication.

I was on the drug for a week when I either had a reaction to it or a spiritual experience. It happened in the morning and I was still in bed. I'd awakened but my eyes were still closed. I was clearly in my apartment and aware of what was going on around me. Jamal was talking to me but I wouldn't open my eyes and ruin the experience. I was trying to savor the moment. The feeling I had was so real. The emotions it stirred in me were what I'd feel if I didn't have any worries, mainly financial worries. I felt prosperous—very blessed. When I tried to associate my feelings with an experience, I saw myself in a beautiful, spacious home where I was picking out the décor. It was so real that it was like I was sunbathing with my eyes closed. I could feel the atmosphere as if it were radiant heat. I was enveloped in it. I knew I was only getting a taste of it but I didn't want it to end. I was in paradise. Jamal had gotten out of bed and gone into the living room to watch TV. I just lay in the bed and sprawled out like I was floating on a cloud. It was the best feeling but I couldn't relish it indefinitely. Jamal called to me to come watch *Head of State* starring Chris Rock. Talk about a stark contrast to my spiritual high. We'd talked about how funny it was that some of the scenes in the movie, which was made years before, mimicked the obstacles Barack Obama was facing in his run for president. We'd gotten a good laugh from it and the fact that it started coming on television frequently during the campaign. Someone else must have seen the same parallels. I couldn't ignore Jamal forever. When I spoke to him the experience ended. Poof! Just like that it was over.

I didn't tell Jamal about my experience right away. First of all, I had to research my medication to see if I was having a bad trip. I had no idea what had happened to me. I wanted to think of it as a taste of what's to come. I asked myself if I thought it was heaven. Thankfully I didn't think so. I'd imagine if it were heaven I wouldn't have been able to liken it to anything. This experience immediately invoked feelings of earthly prosperity and wellbeing. It wasn't anything otherworldly. I eventually told Jamal that I'd had this feeling of bliss. That's all I could say to describe it. I also told him that I'd be richer than Bill Gates if I could bottle it and sell it.

I've heard of people of other faiths having a bliss experience but it's usually a meditative state. My Protestant religion doesn't really speak about meditation or experiences of this nature so this was all new to me. I'd say I was in a meditative state in the sense that, while I was going through chemo, I always prayed when I was in bed. Sometimes I prayed myself to sleep. I was eager to hear from God and since I was in bed I would just talk to Him and ask Him questions and next thing I knew it would be the morning. Perhaps I'd reached this meditative state before I awakened. Or it could have been a state of euphoria, which was a side effect of my drug. I've never experienced drug-induced euphoria so I had no idea what that would feel like. My mother was on the same drug for her epilepsy and she'd never had anything like that happen to her. Although, I don't think drug-induced euphoria would have been as radiant or would have ended because I'd spoken to Jamal. I'm more inclined to think I had a taste of what's to come in my life.

Some religions aim for their members to reach the state that I haphazardly achieved. From what I've read, it's the goal of meditation. If I indeed reached the same state that meditators reached, I'd say the goal is really for the state to manifest in our everyday lives. I'd argue that, if it's a spiritual state, then it would serve a purpose. I find God to be a God of purpose. I don't think

He does anything just for amusement or for us to get a high. Therefore, I won't be trying to reach bliss again through meditation. However, I'm waiting patiently for the promise of that blissful experience to come to fruition—to see if it was indeed a foreshadowing of what's to come—something to encourage me by showing that things will get better.

CHAPTER TWELVE:
Burn, Baby, Burn

"Everybody wants happiness.
Nobody wants pain but you can't have
a rainbow without a little rain."

–Unknown

pring is my favorite time of year. It's so bright and cheery. Everything comes alive. Trees and shrubs that had green leaves birth brighter green leaves. Fruit-bearing trees start to blossom, tulips and daffodils make their appearance—all to announce brighter days ahead. My birthday is in the spring and I always imagine that all the pretty, colorful flowers are making their debut to celebrate me. I was glad to see the cloudy skies dissipate and sunshine to accompany the rain, bringing pretty rainbows. Literally and figuratively my fall/winter was over. The darkest part of my journey was behind me. Sixteen weeks of chemotherapy were finished. I'd now have radiation daily except on the weekends. It could possibly make me a little tired but it wouldn't be anything like chemo.

I'd heard stories about people with darker skin not doing very well with radiation, which didn't make sense to me. I thought that if we had built in protection from the sun, my extra melanin should help me out.

Radiation was very quick. Nothing like the hours of infusions with chemo. I went in, changed into a gown, they'd call me back, and put me on a machine. Once they got me all lined up (they tattooed me to make sure they shot me in the same place) it lasted about five to ten minutes.

During radiation, the presidential campaign was picking up steam. By this time Barack Obama had won quite a few states and was leading Hillary Clinton in delegates. One particular day I entered the radiology center and as usual the televisions were turned to the news. There were all kinds of pundits on every channel 24/7 talking about the campaign. I was so into watching political news that Jamal thought I was obsessed. He thought I'd surely go into withdrawals once the campaign was over and there was nothing left to talk about. I grabbed a seat next to this older white gentleman who had to be in his late seventies/early eighties and he leaned over to me and said, "We're living in very auspicious times. I think we're going to have our first black president." At the time I didn't know what the hell "auspicious" meant but it sure sounded a lot like suspicious so I thought to myself, *Oh boy, here we go.* There was so much racial tension because of Obama being black. He's actually part white and part Kenyan but no one paid much attention to the white side of him. I think he could have slipped under the radar had he not had a black wife. There was no mistaking that Michelle, Obama's wife, was black, which I think made some white people view him as identifying more with his black side. I think that if he'd had a white wife and his kids were biracial there wouldn't have been as much drama surrounding his candidacy.

If Barack Obama could be elected president of the United States, we would definitely have our first black president, our first black first lady, and our first black first family and that scared some people. So much so that the gentleman I was sitting next to told me that he would love to have a Barack Obama sticker on his car but he wasn't sure how the people in his neighborhood would respond to that. I quickly put two and two together to figure out that "auspicious" meant something good. He said how it was such a shame that he even had to be concerned about something so ridiculous but that he was going to vote for Barack Obama no matter what.

Aside from keeping myself entertained with politics, radiation was pretty uneventful. All I did was come in, get these invisible rays shot at me, and once a week I'd see the doctor so that she could make sure I was responding well to the radiation—not burning or anything. If I did start burning they'd stop my treatments for a while so that I wouldn't burn too badly.

Michelle was my last sister to visit. She's the quintessential middle child in that she was the mischievous one who never thought she fit in. My mom told me that she'd run away at the age of three. How a three year old thinks to run away and how my mom didn't realize she had left is beyond me but that's how the story goes. She ran to some neighbor lady's house that I don't think my parents even knew. Michelle and I are often told we look a lot alike. We're constantly being mistaken for each other. My fondest memory with Michelle is when I rented the movie *Beaches* years ago. She complained about watching it with me saying that the synopsis sounded boring. I told her that it was a good movie and that she would like it. After a little coaxing she decided to watch it, although she complained a little throughout. Toward the end, when Bette Midler's friend dies and Bette is singing "Wind Beneath My Wings" the two of us were bawling. We looked at each other and busted out laughing. I was right and she was wrong. *Beaches* was a good movie.

I think radiation was the best thing for Michelle to support me through. She can be emotional and I think seeing me connected to IV's surrounded by washed out, sick, older people would have been too much for her. She came to visit my birthday weekend and I had a list of fun stuff planned for us.

Jamal stayed with his parents in Stockton that weekend since it was closer to Sacramento. He was preparing to go to jail for ninety days to serve time for the prior DUI. Jamal always came across as big and bad but serving ninety days in jail with hardened criminals scared him. He was moody and drinking a lot because of it. I'm sure jail is no cakewalk but I felt like "you do the crime, you pay the time". I just wanted him to man up. He really wanted me to feel sorry for him but I couldn't. Hell! I was fighting for my life and I wasn't falling apart.

Jamal definitely had some hurdles to overcome but they paled in comparison to what I was going through in my opinion and I had very little sympathy for him. I don't mean to sound insensitive but it was probably because I felt his drinking and moodiness showed very little sympathy for what I was going through. Not to mention I had been chauffeuring him back and forth to work, to and from lunch at his insistence, to his appointments with his attorney, and anywhere else he needed to go. That wasn't exactly how I expected to spend my long term disability and I didn't feel he was appreciative of my sacrifice. He was being more of a burden than a help and I was looking forward to some time apart.

It's funny because sometimes I'd ask myself, *Are you sure this was a blessing from God?* Now I understand that just because God blesses you with something doesn't mean that blessing comes without responsibility. If God blesses you with a house, you still have to clean the house. If God blesses you with a child, that child might go through a terrible teens phase but it doesn't mean that the child isn't a blessing. I felt our marriage was a blessing but it would still take a lot of effort on our parts to make it work.

I'd never been to Alcatraz so I thought taking Michelle there would be fun. We drove to the city and then took a ferry over to the island. It was a nice day but it wasn't hot. Still, I was having hot flashes and sweating like a whore in church, which made me self-conscious and probably made me sweat even more. I was miserable.

While we were touring the jail cells I couldn't help but think of my husband. He was going to jail for ninety days but I sure hoped he wouldn't serve any hard time for the embezzlement charge because of some fluke. You can be innocent of something but it doesn't necessarily mean that the prosecution can't make a believable case against you. So far, we'd been able to get his trial postponed due to my cancer but we were nearing the time that his attorney would need to present his case. This attorney, who we'd thought was so great, turned out to be super busy and gave us the impression that Jamal's case wasn't high profile enough for him to take seriously. Jamal was getting concerned because some of the witnesses that he felt could really corroborate his story hadn't been contacted by his attorney. He also didn't feel like the attorney fully understood his job in order to understand how impossible it was for him to do what his former employer was accusing him of. Jamal having to put his future in someone else's hands who he thought didn't really take him seriously just added to his stress.

With all that I was going through, my sister's visit was a welcome distraction. Michelle and I had a great time in the city sightseeing and shopping. The following day I planned to take her to Napa for my birthday. I hadn't seen my sister in a while and having had such an inauspicious (if you will) last few months I just wanted to cherish our time together. We drove out to Napa early enough to tour some of the wineries, have lunch at a nice restaurant and then have a vineyard tour and sparkling wine tasting at Mumm. Notice that I said sparkling wine and not champagne. Champagne can only be called champagne if it was produced in France's Champagne Region. Napa is very beautiful but I must admit it's hard to be enamored when you've visited *the* Champagne Region. I'd been to Reims and Épernay, notable champagne producing towns in France, a few times and every time I absolutely loved it. There's so much history there. Some of the champagne caves have been there since the 1700s. I loved how every restaurant or café I visited had stainless champagne buckets with several bottles of champagne chilling. It's like they're in celebration mode 24/7—ready to pop a bottle if you just say the word. Love it! I visited Veuve Clicquot, Moet, and Piper Heidsieck, to name a few. I did love visiting Mumm in Napa though. The tasting salon has a very scenic view of the vineyards and they have a nice presentation. There are some great wines in Napa. I had a marvelous birthday and was thrilled that Michelle was able to share it with me.

Radiation really wasn't having that negative of an effect on me. I was able to ease back into my job by working from home for the last few weeks of my radiation. I had decided to physically go back to work after all of my treatments were complete.

A few weeks before my treatments ended I noticed that my skin, in the areas where I had radiation, was turning really dark and becoming thin. My technician kept remarking how well I was doing and how surprised she was because she'd heard that people with dark skin didn't react that well to radiation. I didn't realize that the reason my skin was getting so dark was because it was burning. Radiation actually still works in your body after your treatments end so a couple of weeks following the last treatment my skin started to peel and reveal pink flesh underneath. It didn't hurt at all but it sure looked painful. I finally had to resort to getting some burn bandages and taping them under my soon-to-be breast and underarm. The burns were huge. The one under my arm was about two by three inches and the one under my breast was about one by three inches and they oozed to the point where I had to change my bandages constantly.

When I finally visited my radiologist, she was surprised by how large my burns were. Because of my dark skin I don't think it was as obvious to them that I was burning as it would have been if I had fairer skin. She recommended that I buy an astringent powder called Domeboro to use as a soak for my burns and change my bandages regularly. Since my treatments were over and I was back at work, it became difficult to care for my wounds. First of all I had on clothes and a bra which sat right on top of my burns. The burn under my arm secreted so much fluid that one day my shirt actually got soiled. I wound up having to start working from home again so that I could soak my wounds regularly and let them get some air. I'd just wear a sarong wrapped around my body so that I didn't have any added friction against the wounds. It was a nice time of year so I'd take my laptop out on my balcony, sit in my lounge chair, and take in the view of the hillside. Not a bad work environment.

Once I started using the Domeboro, the wounds really started to become more manageable. Memorial Day approached and I wanted to go to Dallas to visit my sister, Teressa. Dallas was like a home away from home for me. I'd spent a lot of time there prior to going to Paris and after returning. I'd had hopes of living in Dallas after leaving Paris but didn't find a job so I returned to Seattle to live with my parents. I hadn't been to Dallas for several months and I figured I'd take advantage of the three day weekend. I wouldn't dare take vacation after being off of work for almost six months.

This was my first flight since I'd had my lymph nodes removed. I had to take certain precautions to make sure I didn't get lymphedema. I'd been fitted with a compression sleeve shortly after my mastectomy. I have to wear it whenever I fly to prevent my arm from swelling to the size of a small woman's thigh due to the decrease in air pressure. It sounds impossible for an arm to swell that much but I saw a woman on TV with lymphedema and it's not a good look.

I was scheduled to fly out of San Francisco Airport through Las Vegas the Friday before Memorial Day. Naturally, being a three day weekend, it was a pretty busy travel time. When I got to the gate the attendant announced over the loudspeaker that the airline would give a round trip travel voucher for anywhere the airline flew within the contiguous U.S. if passengers were willing to give up their seats. There were too many people trying to go to Vegas for the long weekend. Booking a flight through Las Vegas over the holidays was probably not a good idea. I quickly volunteered to give up my seat. A few of my trips to Paris were made possible by my getting bumped. Although back then they gave you vouchers for round trip tickets anywhere the airline flies. Nowadays you're lucky if they offer you a flight voucher. I've had offers for $200 off of your next flight, which isn't worth the hassle. The attendant promised me they would "take care of me" and get me on the next flight out. But after waiting for two hours for the next flight they took it upon themselves to tell me that I couldn't get on that flight either. They offered to get me on the next "next flight," which wouldn't get me in until after midnight and they had the nerve to not offer me anything to get bumped again. I was pissed! I didn't hesitate to remind them that I'd done them a favor and they'd promised to "take care of me." I told them that I wasn't giving up my seat again without another flight voucher. At first they tried to say they couldn't give me another voucher but I insisted that they could. They called around to make it happen and I ended up with two flight vouchers. Honestly, I wasn't in any hurry to get to Dallas. I was originally scheduled to get there after eight p.m. anyway. We didn't have any plans once I arrived so being delayed a little wasn't a big deal. But I wasn't about to be inconvenienced for free and I surely wasn't going to let them hold me hostage now that I'd given up my seat.

When I reached my sister's house I was greeted by her toy poodle, Fiona. Her full name is actually Fiona Renee Taylor. People always laugh because she has a middle name. I wasn't sure if she'd remember me since I hadn't seen her in almost a year, but she did. True to her character she started licking me like crazy, which always annoyed me. The funny thing was I didn't mind it. It actually felt good. I guess I'd been through so much that it had softened me some.

Maybe Fiona could sense that I'd been through a lot or maybe she'd missed me. I'm not sure what was going on, but that night for the first time ever Fiona got into bed with me and didn't leave until morning. All the times I'd been to my sister's house Fiona had never slept with me. She always slept with my niece, Kiara, or with Teressa and her husband, Wendell. It was just amazing to me that she had such a keen sense of awareness and gave me a little extra love. It made me think about getting a dog of my own. Jamal wasn't big on cuddling like he was during our honeymoon phase so it would be nice to have a cuddly little dog to snuggle with.

I was looking forward to seeing Caryn while I was in Dallas since she lived there. It had taken her a while to find a job after returning from Paris as well. Having been raised in Dallas, she was hoping to find a job outside of Texas or even the U.S. but things hadn't worked out that way. Almost a year after returning, she had found a great job with one of the world's top consumer packaged goods companies so she wasn't doing too badly. We always commiserated about the job hunt and how things were so different from how we'd imagined they would be. One of the great things about being a student is the ability to be so naively optimistic. In some cases things work out better than planned but in a lot of cases, especially in today's environment, finding a job can be challenging. All in all, we both landed decent jobs. They weren't the dream jobs we were expecting but we were building our skillset.

Saturday morning Caryn came to the house. Teressa, Kiara, Caryn, and I were planning on going to the mall. It seems like there are malls and restaurants on every corner in Dallas. I swear, all Dallasites must do is eat and shop. I was still getting dressed when Caryn arrived. I'd sent pictures of my burns to my sister so she kind of knew what they looked like but Caryn hadn't seen them. Neither of them had seen what my breast was looking like so far. I invited them into my room to help me finish getting dressed.

"I still need to apply my soak and bandages before I put on my bra. I just have to mix the powder with water and soak some gauze in it and let the gauze sit on my burns for a few minutes. Then I put some non-stick gauze on the burns and secure them with bandage tape" I showed them how I dressed my wounds and they quickly and graciously helped me.

"Wow! Those are some big burns." Caryn said.

"I know. They look more painful than they are. They don't hurt." I said. Caryn and Teressa couldn't believe all that I'd been subjected to and just cringed at the sight of my burns.

"You are so strong sister." Teressa said and she gave me a big hug.

It was challenging to apply the soak and dress the wound under my arm by myself. Having Teressa and Caryn play nurse on me was so special. They also made sure my wig was looking fabulous since I usually just had to trust my gut. We did a little shopping, ate dinner, and then called it a day. The rest of my time was spent visiting with my Aunt Mary and hanging with my sister. My stay in Dallas was short but sweet. I left on Memorial Day and had no problems flying home. I really enjoyed being with my sister and family. I had gone through this whole battle with just the occasional visit or just talking to them on the phone. Jamal and his family did what they could for me but there's nothing like being with the people who know you best.

Karla's Column

Date: Wed, 16 Apr 2008 09:48 a.m.

From: Michelle@email.com

Subject: The Trip...

To: karla@email.com; teressa@email.com

Dear Sisters,

Hi!!! TT, I know you missed me...LOL Yep, I stayed until Tuesday so I could get my money's worth for the trip. Okay, it was KK's Birthday but she spoiled me. It was really a shame...She did make me sing the birthday song to her in the restaurant (which she totally deserves and I didn't mind). I'm glad she didn't make me sing in French. I would have really stunk the place up...But it was cute.

KK is so beautiful (inside and out). I will never know how she does it. She is taking good care of herself plus she's even motivated to get up in the morning and work on her job...IMAGINE THAT. She could just lay around and do nothing but the girl gets up and starts working like she is actually going into the office...LOL I think I got more sleep than her...lol

Anyway, we had a GLORIOUS time. We really missed you.

I didn't want to go home but of course I had to return to my child and my puppy.

I returned to find that both are well and doing fine. So, they survived but in the future I don't think I can take any more trips.

Hi KK, sorry I didn't let you know I made it home safe because it got late and I didn't want to take a chance of waking you.

I will send b-day pictures this evening.

Write...

Love,

Shell

From: Karla (karla@email.com)

Re: The Trip

Sent: Wed 4/16/08 3:27 PM

To: Michelle (michelle@email.com);
          Teressa (teressa@email.com)

Awww! What a sweet email! Everyone missed you today at radiation. They said what a sweet sister you have. :o) I'm glad my sisters all got to take part in my treatment and recovery. TT we decided Shell was best to come for radiation because she probably wouldn't have been able to take the chemo. LOL. She would have been crying. But I'm doing well bless God! I'm glad it's almost over.

Well love you guys! I've gotta get some work done.

Smooches!

Karla

From: karla@email.com

To: mom@email.com; michelle@email.
          com; teressa@email.com; karla@
          email.com

Subject: My Burns

Date: Fri, 16 May 2008 21:31:19

Here are pics of my burns. They look worse than they are (meaning they don't hurt). I think the most appalling thing about these pics is my double chin. Let's blame it on the way I shot the pictures.

Karla

From: Teressa (teressa@email.com)

Re: My Burns

Sent: Mon 5/19/08 5:37 AM

To: Karla (karla@email.com);
          Edna (mom@email.com);
          Michelle (michelle@email.com)

Oh Sister, you are so STRONG! I'm glad they don't hurt like they look because they look very painful. I can't wait to see you so I can give you some love! Hang in there sister you are a SURVIVOR! Praise be to GOD!

Love you all sisters!

TT~

CHAPTER THIRTEEN:
My New Normal

"Do not pray for an easy life, pray for the strength to endure a difficult one."

--Bruce Lee

*T*he longest six months of my life had passed. I'd finally finished all of my treatments and was seeing Dr. Scott for my post-treatment visit. She walked into the room and gave me a big hug and said "Congratulations! You're done with treatment!"

"I know! I can hardly believe it. It seems like it's taken forever."

"Yeah, you did great though. You only had to come in for that one episode. Other than that you responded really well. The good news is that you're NED. There's no evidence of disease!"

"That's awesome! So what now?" I knew we weren't saying goodbye. This was just the beginning of a long relationship.

"Well you'll come in once a quarter so we can make sure you're still doing well. You'll see me regularly for the next five years. I'll start you on Tamoxifen after your reconstruction and you'll take that for five years as well."

"Oh great! Those damn hot flashes again." I lamented.

"Yes, hot flashes again but think of it this way. They're keeping you alive." She said.

"Okay." I sighed. "I'll try to stay positive."

"You're going to have a new normal. Your body has been through a lot and you might notice some differences because of it. A little ache here or there. There are things you'll want to start doing like working out at least thirty minutes a day, five days a week. You'll want to lose the extra weight you gained during treatment because fat produces estrogen and estrogen is bad for you. The other thing is to keep your stress down. How's everything at home?" She said with a concerned look on her face. Dr. Scott was aware that my marriage was challenging. I'd told her early on that we were going through a legal battle and that Jamal wouldn't be able to accompany me to my appointments because 1) he couldn't drive due to his past DUIs and 2) he wouldn't be able to take much time off from work. She knew that I was playing chauffeur and that he was drinking a lot. However, she didn't know that he was in jail at the time. Jamal wanted to keep that as private as possible.

"Uh. It's okay." I said. In other words "so so".

"Okay. Well we want to keep your risk of recurrence down so all the things I mentioned will help you do that. You should also limit your alcohol intake. Remember you have to take care of yourself."

"Okay. Will do."

Before Dr. Scott left the exam room she gave me another big hug and congratulated me. I was so happy! I was NED (no evidence of disease). Some refer to it as in remission but before I ever had cancer I'd always thought remission sounded like someone was okay...for now. NED sounds more like you are cured. I wouldn't be able to officially consider myself cured until my five year checkup. Five years is the window of time when breast cancer is most likely to recur. For the following five years I'd have quarterly checkups, annual mammograms, and the occasional PET scan.

Living in my new normal meant I'd notice some long term effects of the chemo. I definitely felt like my body had aged. One thing I noticed is that the muscle tone and strength that I'd gained prior to being diagnosed was gone. Muscle atrophy is a temporary side effect of Taxol. Sometimes during my Taxol treatments, if I sat on the couch I'd need Jamal to help me get up. I just didn't have the leg strength. Not keeping up with my exercise regimen probably didn't help. When I tried to work out after a few chemo treatments and my heart started racing I decided to give it a rest.

I knew that most people gained weight after breast cancer treatment so I tried to watch what I ate (when I did feel like eating). I'd already been slightly overweight when I was diagnosed so I didn't want to gain too much more weight. However, in between being diagnosed and starting chemo I went on this "life is short" kick and gained ten pounds. I wasn't about to worry about my weight when I was trying to figure out if I had cancer and what my prognosis was. It was when I started chemo that I decided to eat a little better so that I wouldn't gain more weight and to provide my body with the nutrients it needed. I managed to only gain another ten pounds during treatment, which was less than the average of twenty five pounds. I was still under two hundred pounds. That was my limit. I never wanted to go over two hundred. I always thought of two hundred pounds as going too far. I have a fat gene in my family. Everybody is big. Mostly on my mom's side though. My Grandma Reed was a shapely,

larger woman with an hourglass figure. My mom was shaped the same. I remember my mom would show my sisters and me this picture of her when she was a teenager wearing tight jeans. She was posing in the front yard of my grandparents' house with a rake. She said she'd go out to rake the yard but she was so fine that all the boys in the neighborhood would volunteer to do the yard work for her. How much truth there is to that story I don't know but she did have a nice figure. She actually had more up top than me so she was pretty voluptuous. Now? She's umm... how would you say...plump.

For as long as I can remember, (even when I was slim) I've been watching my weight and I didn't want to watch it top the scale. Dr. Scott suggested that I not worry about my weight during treatment since my body was going through so much but treatment was over now and it was time to get the weight off.

Post-treatment was an exciting time! I was literally going through a rebirth or metamorphosis. Everything was new. My hair, eyelashes, eyebrows, and nails started to grow. My hair felt like a newborn baby's hair. It was really soft and fine. Nothing like the coarse, kinky stuff that had fallen out. I was sure that, with a little time, it would get coarser and it did. My tongue and palms started to turn pink again. I also got my period back and my hot flashes started to subside. Just like the trees and flowers were blossoming in the spring, I was blossoming, and soon I'd have two breasts again.

I must say it was nice not having a period for a while but I was glad to see it come back. Sometimes treatment causes early menopause and Jamal and I were still hoping to have kids. Dr. Scott said that I could take Tamoxifen for two years and then take a break to have a baby and get back on Tamoxifen for the remaining three years. Tamoxifen is typically prescribed for five years straight. Dr. Scott had other patients who were young like me and had had babies after chemo, so I was hopeful that I could do the same.

So I was back to buying tampons and razors and officially back at work since my wounds were healed. Everyone was really glad to have me back. I'd been frustrated with my employer for a lot of reasons but my boss was very supportive and understanding with all of the time off I'd needed. My clients were very supportive as well. They'd sent me flowers and cards while I was out. I'd seen Diane and another co-worker, Naomi, on a regular basis while I was on medical leave. We would meet at the Peet's coffee connected to my apartment and sometimes Naomi would bring me bottled water and meals. My clients felt more like my co-workers because I was in the office with them every day, whereas my boss and colleagues were in Chicago and New York.

Even though I was back at work I'd still need to take another week off to have my reconstructive surgery. I needed to let the radiation run its course and let my body recover so I thought August would be a good time of year to have the surgery. Until that was completed I was still dealing with the effects of cancer. In the spirit of Humpty Dumpty, I wasn't going to feel like I was put back together again until I had a breast. Jamal would also be home by August so I wouldn't be alone.

I picked up Jamal from jail the day he was released. I'd visited him on the weekends (except for when I went to Dallas to visit my family) and made sure he had money in his jail account. I'd sent him inspirational books hoping he'd read them and come out a changed man. I also wanted to keep him encouraged because I knew being locked up could be demoralizing.

Ninety days was a long time to be apart from your spouse. There was so much he'd missed. He hadn't seen my burns or my new baby fine hair. We hadn't hugged or kissed since he'd left. We couldn't touch when we saw each other outside in the courtyard and there was glass separating us in the visitation room.

When Jamal saw me he smiled and let out a big sigh of relief. He gave me the biggest hug and kiss. He collected his personal items and we headed to the car.

"You did it babe!" I told him.

"I'm so glad that's over! I don't ever want to go back to that place."

"Good. I don't ever want you to go back. I sure won't be visiting you if you do." I laughed but was very serious about what I'd said. He responded with a fake laugh. He didn't think what I said was funny not because he planned to go back to jail but because he felt my comment showed a lack of support.

"So how are you babe?"

"I'm doing well. My burns have healed and I can't wait to show you my hair."

"Good. You look good."

"Why thank you! I have my reconstruction in a few weeks. I'm so excited. I'm tired of being lopsided."

"Just a few more weeks and you'll be done."

"Yep. Can't wait!"

Jamal and I caught up. He told me all about the things that transpired in jail. Although he dreaded going in, I don't think it was as bad as he'd imagined. He's pretty street smart and I think he knew how to conduct himself in such a way that he could stay out of trouble. I was glad he'd served his time and we could put that part of his ordeal behind us. As part of his sentence he'd still have to do some community service hours. Then he could go through the process of getting his driver's license back.

I think the time apart was good for us. We both had ninety days of absence to make our hearts grow fonder. Although Jamal frustrated me at times, he was fun to be around when he wasn't in a funk. Now that the jail time was over I was hoping that he'd be in a better mood. Serving time was a huge stressor for him. He was concerned that he might not have a job when he got out but thankfully his employer was nice enough to hold his position for him. Next on his agenda was taking care of the embezzlement case.

I was so excited to have my reconstructive surgery but at the same time I was worried that I wouldn't like the results. I think, after dealing with so many treatments and side effects, that I was hoping the surgery would turn out the way I'd planned. Nothing in the past few months had gone smoothly. I was praying this would be different and I could walk away from this with some nice symmetrical D cups.

Just like before, Dr. Galani came in prior to the surgery with his magic marker. This time my right breast got some love too since I'd finally be getting a lift on that side. Then, my favorite specialist, the anesthesiologist, came in to discuss what kind of drugs I'd have. I made sure to tell him about the bad experience I had coming out of anesthesia during my mastectomy. I didn't want that to happen again. The doctor assured me that my anesthesia wouldn't wear off too soon this time.

I kissed Jamal and they wheeled me into the operating room. The last thing I remember prior to waking up was small talking with the nurse. I was told that my surgery had gone well and after I totally came out of my anesthesia I was released to go home.

My breasts were bandaged and bound so I couldn't really see what they looked like. I'd have to wait for my one week checkup when I'd get my bandages off to really see the full effect. I peeked a little bit and was pleased with what I saw. I had a little cleavage again.

I went into my follow up appointment anxiously awaiting the reveal. Dr. Galani entered the exam room and gingerly removed the surgical tape from my breasts. He stepped back to get a good look at them and said "I'm very pleased with the results."

"Hmmm. They still look a little lopsided to me."

"You just need to wait a few months for the swelling of your right breast to go down and when we add the nipple to the left breast it will protrude a little more."

I didn't think a nipple would make that much of a difference but I took his advice. More waiting but I was getting closer.

I went home and tried on my little tube top sundress without a bra. It was so exciting! Nothing was sagging. I wasn't fighting gravity. My breasts weren't swinging like pendulums. It was great! My right breast protruded a little more than the left (just like before my mastectomy) but this was progress.

Now that my surgery was over, Dr. Scott wanted to start me on Tamoxifen. I wasn't at all enthused about it. All I could think of was getting those damn hot flashes back again. They'd messed with my quality of life before. If I'd just had hot flashes and glistened a little I would be fine. But I sweat profusely and it was so annoying and uncomfortable. Dr. Scott told me that if the hot flashes worsened they could try to treat them but she wanted me to take the Tamoxifen. She really felt it would decrease my risk of recurrence and I'd had so many lymph nodes involved that she didn't want me to take any chances. So I started Tamoxifen and also started taking Coumadin, a blood thinner to counteract the effects of Tamoxifen. Tamoxifen can cause blood clots and I have low protein S, an anticoagulant protein, which I inherited from my mom's side of the family. Remember that both my uncle and my grandmother died of embolisms. Dr. Scott also wanted me to start taking calcium and vitamin D, which have also been linked to reducing breast cancer risk.

Once I had my breasts for a while I wasn't sure that they were going to work. The left one was kind of flat. It looked fine in a tube top summer dress when both of my breasts were flattened but when I put on a bra it wasn't filling it in properly. It needed a little more than a nipple to make it symmetrical. I still had to put a pad in my bra to make it balance with the right breast and that wasn't what I'd had in mind. I knew I'd gone into the surgery with lopsided breasts but I wasn't going to pay for lopsided breasts and the law stipulates that I could have symmetry. How hard could that be? I knew I didn't have two real breasts but I didn't think I had to have low expectations. I talked to Dr. Galani about my concerns and the problem of the implant being flat. It didn't protrude. There is an implant that has more of a teardrop shape but according to Dr. Galani you can only get them in Mexico. Dr. Galani and I decided that we would revisit the situation in the New Year. After all my body had been through he didn't recommend having another surgery so soon. In the meantime, he would think of what my options were.

Right about that time I wished I had some options when it came to Tamoxifen. Those damn hot flashes were kicking my ass. It was seriously debilitating for me. I was so young and they weren't something that is expected at my age. It really made me feel like I was still sick. When I broke into a sweat I had to explain to people that I was on medication that caused me to have hot flashes. If it weren't for the hot flashes I would have felt normal. I had little aches and pains sometimes but it was the hot flashes that made me feel miserable. They drew so much attention to me. I'd be in a meeting at work and I'd start fanning myself. Everyone would look at me and ask if I was okay. That shit was for the birds! I saw Dr. Scott and she said that she could put me on a low dose anti-depressant. It could help with the hot flashes. It wouldn't make them go away but it would reduce the frequency and duration, which was better than nothing.

September rolled around and Jamal's son, J.J., came to visit for the first time since we'd remarried. J.J. has cerebral palsy and is in a wheelchair. He was choked by his umbilical cord during delivery. J.J. and his mom live in New York. Jamal hadn't seen him because of all that was going on with his legal issues and my health. Now that Jamal's jail time and my treatment were out of the way we'd thought it was a good idea for J.J. to come to California. Being disabled J.J. requires a lot of care. Jamal was able to take off a few days for his visit. We planned a birthday barbeque for him. He's just like his dad in that he loves to swim. Jamal's parents have a nice backyard with a pool so he could swim to his heart's content. I even decided to swim. It was a nice, beautiful day so I peeled off the wig and took a dip. I was still wearing wigs since my hair hadn't totally grown out yet. I'd gone through my natural hair phase and was over it. I suppose I could have gotten braids but I hate how they pull on my scalp. My hair was getting thicker but I didn't want to cut it or do anything to it until I felt it had gotten past that new, fine hair stage and it was actually the texture of mature hair. I looked pretty good up top in my swimsuit. If you looked at my breasts too long you could probably tell something was amiss but I was amongst family and friends so I wasn't too worried about it.

They all knew I was being reconstructed.

Swimming was a blast but I noticed that one area in the back of my scalp was a little itchy afterwards. The hair in that area started to break off in the subsequent days. I had a little bald patch in the back of my head. That was a little bit of a setback in my hair growth. I'd been hoping to let my hair grow long enough that when I went in for a relaxer I could get a cute, short cut. Now I was either going to have to style my hair around a bald patch or wait for the area to heal and grow hair before I could get my hair relaxed. I went to a dermatologist who told me that I had seborrheic dermatitis. Chlorine can exacerbate the symptoms so I'd probably had it all along and kicked it into overdrive by going swimming. The doctor recommended that I delay getting a relaxer and he prescribed some shampoo and a topical treatment. I'd just have to wear my wigs a little longer. This experience is really teaching me to have patience.

Survivorship: Year Two

CHAPTER FOURTEEN:
There's a First Time for Everything

**"Life isn't about waiting for the storm to pass.
It's about learning to dance in the rain"**

--Unknown

*I*t had been a year since I'd had my mastectomy and I didn't have a completed reconstruction and was still wearing wigs. It had been a long process that I wasn't sure I'd been prepared for when told I had cancer. The weeks just add up because you can't do everything straight through. I'd had surgery, followed by a few weeks to recover from that, then sixteen weeks of chemotherapy, and a few weeks to recover from that, then six weeks of daily radiation, and a few weeks to recover from that, reconstruction, and time to recover from that.

It was Breast Cancer Awareness month again and just like last year my client was participating in the annual City of Hope Breast Cancer Walk in San Francisco. I got the feeling that since

I was a survivor now everyone expected me to walk. I didn't want to disappoint. Besides I was proud to be a survivor. I could have shouted it from the rooftops. The last time I'd registered as a survivor in faith because all I had was a diagnosis. I hadn't had my mastectomy or anything. This time I knew what it meant to be a survivor.

All of the survivors were supposed to go to a special booth and have their pictures taken so they could assemble the pictures into a big, pink ribbon. They took my name and how many years I'd been a survivor. Naturally, the people at the survivor booth couldn't believe I was a survivor and that I'd had breast cancer as recently as the year before. I felt like I could be a good poster child on doing breast self-exams. *This could happen to you.*

Jamal and I finished the walk in record time and unlike the previous year we had breakfast at a nice restaurant on Embarcadero afterwards. The previous year, we'd walked past all of these great restaurants but didn't go back and eat. This year we decided that we would enjoy the scenery a little more. It was a beautiful day and I was feeling pretty triumphant. Enjoying a nice omelet and mimosa while overlooking the water was a great reward for finishing the 5K.

A few weeks later, there was another breast cancer walk in San Jose that was put on by the American Cancer Society. This one was on the anniversary of my mastectomy, October 25th, which is the day I consider to be my first day cancer-free. I don't normally sign up for these walks on my own but this walk coincided with such a milestone day for me that I couldn't resist signing up. Diane agreed to come along to San Jose and walk with me. I didn't want to wear the black jogging suit I'd worn to the City of Hope walk. I knew everyone at the American Cancer Society walk would be in pink and I didn't want to look like I was in mourning. None of my other jogging suits were suitable colors so I went out and bought a pair of gray workout pants to complement my pink American Cancer Society t-shirt. They were a little clingy but I figured my t-shirt would camouflage my junk in the trunk.

Diane and I finished the walk fairly quickly so we thought we'd visit the booths that were set up around the finish line. They were the typical booths where companies offered free food and drinks or provided educational information. For example, one booth had the fat contents of foods in little pouches to give the visual of what you're doing to your body when you eat junk food. It looked like the stuff you see sucked into a jar (minus the blood) when you watch a liposuction on one of those plastic surgery shows. One that caught my attention was the fat content in a McDonald's value meal. Who couldn't relate to that? It was pretty eye opening. I never looked at a value meal the same way.

After stopping by a few booths, Diane and I stopped in front of the eight pink ladies the American Cancer Society had on display to symbolize the one in eight women who would be diagnosed with breast cancer that year. It seemed kind of theme park-ish but I wanted to take a picture in front of it. We found a nice gentleman to take a good head to toe picture of us. When the two of us reviewed the picture I was appalled. "Oh my God! Look how big my hips and ass are! You have to crop that out."

"What are you talking about? You look great!"

"Look at all of that! I think if we make it a bust shot it will be just fine."

Diane being the sweet, supportive friend that she is cropped the picture right away. Maybe it was a bad angle that made my hips and ass look extra big or maybe it was those workout pants or maybe I'd just had too many McDonald's value meals. Whatever the case, I needed to get serious about losing weight.

Election Day came soon after the ACS breast cancer walk. I took the day off because I didn't want to miss anything. I also wanted to volunteer and play a role in making history. I went to my local Obama for America office and teamed up with other volunteers to knock on doors and make sure people got out to the polls. I got up really early and cast my vote. The lines were long because there was a lot at stake. Senator Obama was running with Senator Joe Biden, a well-known senator from Delaware. Senator John McCain had won the Republican nomination and was running with the first term governor of Alaska, Sarah Palin. Sarah Palin, although she was the governor of Alaska and had been in politics for a few years, was no Hillary Clinton. It seemed she was in a bubble in Alaska and for that reason was not well versed in international relations, geography, history, or any other subject in which you would want someone who would be one heartbeat away from the presidency to be well versed. She couldn't name publications that she reads on a regular basis or any notable Supreme Court rulings. Apparently, she didn't know that Africa is a continent and not a country. She spoke in a very folksy manner. If you hear her speak it's like she's reading a bedtime story—her speech is very animated. And she wasn't at all what she appeared to be. She preached abstinence and Christianity but the day they announced she would be running on the ticket with John McCain her daughter came out on the stage hiding an out of wedlock pregnancy. The Right Wing loved her though. She was very outdoorsy, knew how to shoot a rifle, she waved a flag, said "patriot" and "maverick" a lot, and she was attractive. She was a breath of fresh air to them. They didn't care that she was ditzy. I've heard people say that the American people are not very intelligent and during this election I understood what they meant. I can't believe people would play with our lives like that.

There were so many other, more qualified people that John McCain could have chosen but he and his camp thought that Sarah Palin would appeal to a group of people that he wasn't reaching. It boiled down to who could help him win, not who was the most qualified.

It was pretty scary—the thought of Sarah Palin being president—which you had to take into consideration because John McCain was old and had had a couple of run-ins with skin cancer. If you weren't sure if you wanted to vote for Obama, I'm pretty sure the thought of Sarah Palin being president was enough to get you to the polls. Voter turnout was the highest it had been in forty years. Men and women, young and old, waited in line for hours just to cast their votes. People all over the nation were excited about the very realistic possibility that we would have our first black president and that he would change the way Washington was run. We were so exhausted by 9/11, the war in Iraq, and the war in Afghanistan that we just wanted to move in a different direction.

I knocked on doors in an affluent area of Dublin and to my surprise the white folks who opened the doors were gung-ho about going to the polls to vote for Obama. Most of them had already cast their votes or were getting ready to. The people whose homes Obama for America sent us to were registered Democrats so that probably helped.

After volunteering I went home to watch the votes come in. Jamal and I had some bubbly chilling so that we could have a toast when Senator Obama became president. We switched between news channels to hear all of the commentators and

pundits discuss counties and states whose votes were being tal-
lied. When Senator Obama won a few states that had previously voted for Bush and that McCain needed in order to win, like
Virginia, Ohio, and Florida, it was pretty evident that Obama
was sitting pretty. But we had to wait for the West coast polls to
close and for Obama to reach the coveted 270 electoral votes.
Leading up to the West coast polls closing Obama only needed
fifty more electoral votes. California counts for fifty-five electoral votes by itself and is historically democratic. As soon as
eight o'clock p.m. Pacific Standard Time hit, the news channels
called the election for Obama. Jamal and I cheered and hugged.

It was a great day in America. The nation of slavery, Jim
Crow, and the Civil Rights Movement had elected its first black
president. I was proud as I watched President Elect Obama and
his family walk on stage for him to make his acceptance speech.
Jamal and I lifted our glasses and toasted to the progress we'd
just witnessed and cheered, "Yes we can! Yes we can!" which
was President Obama's rally cry. I was excited that we might
actually see the United States of America with universal health
care or at least laws in place that would prevent patients from
being denied coverage because of pre-existing conditions or
having to mortgage their homes to pay for medical treatment.

The holidays were fast approaching and I hadn't spoken to
Delaine, my chemo buddy, in a few months. I had been thinking
about calling her but just hadn't gotten around to it. We'd spoken regularly when I was going through chemo but after that our
calls got farther and farther apart. One night I went to sleep and
had a dream. It was very short. There was nothing memorable

about the setting. Everything was black. I remember talking to Delaine. Just exchanging a few words. It was like I came into the dream at the end of our conversation. All I remember is that it was implied in the dream that we were commiserating about going through cancer. I must have said something to her because she responded to me, "At least you have more options. They've done everything they can for me."

Shortly after I woke up my sister Michelle called me and said, "Did you hear about Delaine?"

"No. What happened?"

"She's in the hospital. They aren't giving her long. They said there's nothing more they can do for her."

"Oh no. Are you serious? Wow. I just had a dream about her and she told me the same thing. That's such a trip!" I told Michelle the details of the dream.

"That's crazy! She's at Virginia Mason. She's not doing well. She really put up a good fight though. They didn't think she would live this long."

"I know. She helped me get through chemo. I figured if she could go through it so long I could survive sixteen weeks. I'm going to call the hospital. She's been on my mind lately but I just hadn't gotten around to calling. Then I had that dream about her. That's so weird!"

I hung up with Michelle and called the hospital. Virginia Mason is a hospital in Seattle. Apparently, Delaine's in-laws had encouraged her to go back to Seattle to be with her family because she wasn't looking very good. Yalonda, her cousin, thought Delaine had been in denial about her health. When she got to Seattle she looked really sick. Delaine had always been very well put together even at her sickest so it would have been obvious that her health was declining if she was too weak to glam up. The times that I'd spoken to her she'd sounded fine and I guess that was how she'd put everyone at ease who was far away. A few days after she got to Seattle her legs started to swell, which can be a sign in people who are dying that their system is starting to shut down.

Delaine's mom answered the phone at the hospital. When I asked if I could speak to Delaine she said, "She's not coherent. She's leaving us Karla."

"Oh...okay. Is she able to hear?"

"Yes."

"Please tell her thank you for being my inspiration and helping me get through chemo and tell her that I love her."

"I will. Thank you for calling."

Delaine passed away a couple of hours after I called.

I'm not sure why I had that dream. Maybe it was Delaine's way of saying goodbye. In the dream I got the sense that she wasn't ready to go, but since the doctors had already tried everything she had to come to grips with it. We had spoken before about faith and healing and she fully believed that God would heal her. She shared a dream she'd had with me in which she was lying on an operating table and there was this huge, heavy weight on her like a boulder. The weight was removed and she said she felt so much peace. She believed that dream was telling her that she would be healed and she believed it was possible. I shared with her my experience of having a feeling of bliss and that I believed that I would prosper. We'd talked about the goodness of God and our faith in Him and that was the last time I spoke with her. Now she was gone. No healing ever came for Delaine but I'm sure she's experiencing that peace that she dreamt about.

Jamal and I decided to go to New York for Christmas and New Year's to see J.J. We didn't have much money so the fact that one of my clients, James, hooked us up with free housing was a godsend. He was in a bicoastal engagement and his fiancé owned a condo on the Upper West Side of Manhattan, complete with a doorman and concierge. His fiancé was going to join him on the West coast for the holidays and her place would be vacant. All Jamal and I had to do was pay for our flight and bring spending cash. James was a nice guy. He felt I deserved a nice vacation. This would be my first post-treatment, disease-free trip.

I was excited. I'd only been to New York twice before. Once when I was around seven and my parents had taken my sisters and me on a trip to see my dad's side of the family in St. Vincent, then to Puerto Rico and Barbados, and lastly New York to see my grandma. I don't remember much about the New York leg of the trip other than people trying to wash our car windows when we stopped at lights and being in my grandma's apartment. The other time I went to New York was before my grandma died. We went up to Lennox Hill Hospital to visit her once she was diagnosed with cancer. I'd thought that if I had to choose between seeing her alive or attending her funeral I'd rather it be when she was living so I made sure to go with my parents before she died. That was a short trip. We managed to do a little sightseeing between hospital visits. It was shortly after 9/11 so we went to Ground Zero. We also managed to see the Metropolitan Museum of Art, the Natural History museum, and Central Park.

This time our trip would be ten days and I had a full list of sights to see. The first few days we stayed in with J.J. The weather was really cold. It had been snowing and we didn't have a car. J.J.'s mom has a van to transport him but Jamal and I, with no transportation, weren't as comfortable getting him around in New York. J.J. can also catch a cold fairly easily so we didn't want to have him outside too much. Thus we enjoyed a couple of days with J.J. at the condo and then when he left we did some sightseeing.

The big event for the trip was going down to Time Square on New Year's Eve to see the ball drop. We went there a few days prior to scope it out and it was crowded with people. The stage area was set up in preparation for the festivities. Jamal took me to one of his favorite places to hang out in Times Square, ESPN Zone, and we had dinner and a few beers. Then we went to Rockefeller Plaza to see the Christmas tree and ice rink, and next walked over to Radio City Music Hall. One day we went to Harlem, walked around, and had lunch at Sylvia's. Shout out to Sylvia's for the chicken liver that practically melted in my mouth. Yummmm! Another day I took Jamal on a crash sight-seeing tour and wore him out. We went to Ground Zero, the New York Stock Exchange, to see the charging bull in Bowling Green, the Brooklyn Bridge, Chinatown, and Little Italy all in one day.

I'd wanted to go to Chinatown because I'd heard they had really good knock-off designer handbags. I'd always been op-posed to knock-offs. For goodness sake I could have gotten knock-offs in Europe and I resisted then. But one of my girl-friends had a very convincing imitation that made me consider getting one. I thought I'd go see for myself but I hadn't decided if I would buy.

Just walking down the street in Chinatown you are bom-barded by people saying, "watches, Louis Vuitton, Gucci!" as you pass. When the cops drive by they scatter like roaches with the light shining on them or try to look inconspicuous. They have photos of all their handbags. I saw a few people buying them but I tried to act like I was above that. *Do I look like I need to buy a knock-off?* Some of them looked pretty good though.

After I passed a few of the criminals I saw a Louis Wannabe Bag that caught my eye. I caught the fever and succumbed to the wiles of the luxury knock-off pushers. It was like buying drugs or something. I showed them which one I wanted and they took me and Jamal around the corner into an alley-cum-storage area. I bought a Coach wannabe bag for a gift and a Louis Vuitton wannabe for myself. It was a grimy experience but I was proud of myself. I'd gotten over my opposition to knock-offs. I mean no one would know they were fakes. How many times had I seen someone with a knock-off and hadn't known it? Probably umpteen times. If I dressed the part no one would ever think that it wasn't real. Just because I drive an economy car doesn't mean I can't afford a Louis bag. Right?

We saw a lot that day and if it sounds like I was cramming a lot of sightseeing into a few days, I was. This trip enlightened me. I already understood that Jamal and I travel differently. I'd known that but would try to change him in the past. Now I try to understand him. Jamal is content to relax when he is on vacation, whereas I like to see things. So when I have him out I try to get the most out of our time together. Believe me, he was complaining about all of the walking. For me it was no big deal. That's what I did in Paris. You walked everywhere there. There were many days where I would just walk and explore. All that walking in New York City was like old times in Paris for me. Not to mention I was on a mission to see the places I hadn't seen before.

We were both excited about the big New Year's Eve bash at Times Square. We were told people arrive early so we planned to be there at three o'clock. You couldn't bring any bags, food or alcohol. Jamal and I both own flasks but we didn't want to risk them being confiscated so we spiked our Starbucks lattes really good with some Johnnie Walker (compliments of James) before we left. Gotta keep warm right? We were also told that there wouldn't be any restrooms. How you could spend over nine hours without having to go to the bathroom was beyond me. One police officer told us that some people wear diapers. I know. Gross! Right?

It was threatening to snow that day so we made sure to bundle up. When we arrived at Times Square it was already packed with people. It was freezing cold. Fifteen degrees with a little wind and snow flurries from time to time. The weather report said that it was fifteen degrees but felt like one degree. We made friends with people from all over the country. There was a group of Floridians who were huddled together trying to keep warm. We were sure they had to be freezing not being used to the weather. We tried to stay inside a crowd so as to block the wind.

The electric billboard was counting down the hours until midnight. It was when it read five hours to go that I'd had enough. I'd wanted to be at Times Square and see the ball drop but this was ridiculous. I had to pee, my nose was running, my fingers were numb, and I was hungry. After we saw a few people call it quits we decided that our New Year's Eve wouldn't be any less special if we went home. We could say we'd been there. We broke through the barricade and proceeded to leave. On our way to the subway, we noticed one lowly pizzeria that happened to be open for business. Everything else in Times Square was either closed or had a pricey cover charge. Our first order of business was to use the restroom. It was nice and cozy in there and once we relieved ourselves we thought we'd eat there and stay near the festivities, so we had a nice, cheap dinner and entertained ourselves by reveler watching.

We stayed in the restaurant for a few hours. Long enough to

weather the freezing temperatures a little longer so we headed back to the New Year's celebration. The police officers tried to act stern but after a little coaxing they let us back in. There really weren't as many people there as in past years due to the cold weather so they were probably more lenient. The whole affair was being televised and they needed people to make it look festive. We walked around a bit and took pictures with the CNN news crew and then Ludacris took the stage. He was performing his current hit so we stayed to hear him perform. Notice I said hear and not see. I was disappointed to find out that they have a select few people in a reserved area that the camera pans over to make it look like a big crowd. Outside of that area you were reduced to seeing the performance on the Jumbotron because the stage was elevated. When you're at home watching Times Square everything looks so accessible. It's all camera tricks, and they pulled a lot of camera tricks that night to make it look like a lot of people were at Times Square. You'll notice there were few, if any, aerial shots of that New Year's celebration. The next year I noticed the commercials for New Year's Eve at Times Square were showing New Year's Eve 2007 clips instead of New Year's Eve 2008 because there'd been a better turnout.

After the Ludacris performance we decided to leave and ring in the New Year on the rooftop of our borrowed condo. James had given us *carte blanche* on the liquor. They'd just had an engagement party and weren't going to drink all of the leftover alcohol. He'd told me to put a bottle of Perrier-Jouët on to chill earlier that day. How sweet!

We watched CNN when we got home. They were asking viewers to write and tell them how they were spending New Year's Eve and they were showing viewers' pictures on television. I decided to set up a CNN iReport account to tell them that we'd been in Times Square but couldn't tolerate the chill and had decided to go to our rooftop on the Upper West Side and watch the fireworks from there. I sent in a picture of us in our Times Square New Year's Eve hats and lo and behold they mentioned us and included our picture in an online news article.

Just a little before midnight we headed to the rooftop, popped the Perrier-Jouët, watched the fireworks, and toasted to a New Year. I'd never been so happy to say goodbye to a year. Two thousand eight with all of its treatments and side effects had not been my idea of a good year. I was looking forward to putting cancer further and further behind me. Good riddance 2008. Bring on 2009!

A couple of days later, just two days before we were supposed to leave, I wanted to see the Statue of Liberty. Jamal of course was only interested in relaxing so I planned to go alone. I was also planning to go back to Chinatown to buy another bag. I decided to gift the Louis Vuitton Wannabe and get myself the latest tote style Louis Wannabe. I thought it was more practical and I could take it to work. I went straight to the same area I'd been to before and showed them the bag I wanted. They sold it to me for sixty dollars. I tried to talk them down but the guy informed me that it was "Louis Vuitton" as if it were really Louis Vuitton. The knock-offs *are* pretty convincing though. They have tags like a real bag and even come in cloth bags like a real bag. I settled for the price he quoted me, bought the bag, and made my getaway down the subway entrance right next to their post.

You know the saying, all that glitters is not gold? Well when I got back to the condo, I noticed that my glittering gold was turning green, so to speak. That particular tote style has a thin leather drawstring. When it's made of real leather I'm sure the thin drawstring holds up a lot better than the pleather drawstring on my *tromp l'oeil* bag. In places where the bag had been folded to fit into the little cellophane bag they ship it in from China, the drawstring was breaking down and in some places it was broken. I was so pissed but what could I do? I was sure they didn't take refunds or make exchanges. Just like Whitney Houston and her alleged crack purchases there was no receipt. If I hadn't been leaving the next day, I'd have gone back there and given them a piece of my mind. Just like my sister, Teressa, had done when she'd come to visit me in Paris and bought a print from a street vendor outside of Versailles. The artist was passing it off as an original. When we walked down the street a few blocks, I said, "Hey, isn't that your picture?" pointing to a carrousel outside of a gift shop. She said, "It sure is!" We hightailed it back to the gates of Versailles and she told the artist politely in a quiet but threatening voice that she wanted her money back because she saw the same painting down the street. I think she'd paid him about twenty euros. Not to disturb the rest of his business, he quickly gave her her money back. That's what I wanted to do to this hustler who'd swindled me out of my money, touting my bag as a "Louis Vuitton" (as he emphasized). Well the saying is true: you get what you pay for. I had no business stooping to that level anyway. I chalked it up as getting what I deserved and told myself *Let that be a lesson to you.* When I get a Louis Vuitton I want all that comes with it. I want to go into the boutique and receive the best customer service. I don't want to have to look over my shoulder or make a getaway. If something is wrong with it I want to be able to return it. And if someone is staring at it I don't want to wonder if they can tell it's a fake. So that was my knock-off experience and I'm so over it.

The day we were scheduled to leave I woke up with a huge bruise on my leg. I didn't remember bumping into anything so it worried me that the bruise was so large. Flying could cause blood clots, and since I was taking Tamoxifen, which can also cause blood clots, I thought it was a good idea to make sure everything was okay. I was bruising so maybe that meant my blood was too thin. At any rate, I called my doctor and they recommended that I go in to an emergency room to be examined. I took a cab to the nearest hospital, which happened to be the same hospital I'd visited my grandmother in a few years prior. I never thought when I visited her that I would be back at the same hospital for myself.

The ER was full of people and after waiting to be seen for five hours and having to reschedule my flight for the following day, I decided to call my doctor's office to get the read on the last test I'd had to detect my anticoagulant levels. According to them, my blood was so thin that there was no way I could have a clot. Once I got that news and had fixed my own problem I told the hospital I was leaving. Wouldn't you know they sent me a bill for $300 and I wasn't even examined by the doctor?! She'd come out and introduced herself, saw the bruise, and told me someone would come and take my blood but no one ever came. Oh well, it was better to be safe than sorry. We were able to fly home without incident.

A few weeks after I got back from New York, I decided that my scalp had cleared up enough for me to get my first perm. My dermatologist had said I needed to wait six months but that was out of the question. As soon as the hair started to grow back in the affected area, I was ready to get styled.

When I'd first moved to the Bay Area I had no idea where to get my hair done so I decided to go to JC Penney's. I lucked up on the lady I ended up with. She could really do some hair.

I went in with black girl hair and came out with Asian girl hair. My hair was laid and I always got out of there in under two hours. Now she was gone. She was no longer doing hair there and naturally no one knew where she'd gone. I'm sure they were hoping I'd just give another stylist a try but that wasn't happening. My mother-in-law referred me to her hairstylist who was all the way in Stockton. Since I didn't have any other place to go I decided to make an appointment with her. I walked into the salon sporting my short, black wig and when she called me to the chair I revealed my curly, kinky locks. She asked me what style I wanted and I told her I was trying to grow it out so I was aiming for a bob. I didn't know how long my hair would be. It seemed to be about an inch long but, when she put the relaxer on it, it seemed to stretch and stretch. She managed to give me a cute, short bob—tapered in the back to correct for the hair I'd lost. It felt so good to walk out of that salon with my own hair and my wig in my purse. Wigs are great as an option but not so much when they're a necessity. I was glad to be getting back to normal.

The last time I'd had a virgin perm was when I was in Paris. I went to Michel Ricard. I referred Caryn to him too. He was from California originally and Caryn and I would joke that his name was really Michael Richards and he'd tried to fancy it up since he was living in Paris. I went to him when I decided that I no longer wanted a natural. The plan was to grow my hair out but Michel was a little scissor happy, or so it seemed. I think he had Parkinson's or something. He had the shakes so I'm not sure if he cut my hair short because he was correcting for a mistake or if he just liked cutting. Caryn's hair was long and he never cut her hair as much as he did mine. He'd been my hairdresser for about a year. I came to him with short hair and left Paris with short hair. You can imagine how happy I was when I got back to the states and my hair was allowed to grow. At any rate, the virgin perm that Michel had given me had taken a couple of tries to get it totally straight. My new hairdresser in Stockton got it right the first time. This virgin perm was bone straight. It was so pretty and shiny. Happy days were here again!

It was a new year and I'd gotten my hair together, so now all I needed to do was get my breasts fixed up and I'd be good to go. I met with Dr. Galani and he suggested that we put two implants in my left breast, one on top of the other. That should give the projection that I was looking for since we couldn't access a teardrop shaped implant. It sounded promising to me so we scheduled the surgery for early February. By then I was pretty used to being drugged and cut on. The surgery went off without a hitch. The end result was a breast that protruded. However, it was hard as hell. When I hugged people I felt like I was assaulting them. It was like having a doorknob on my chest. The other problem was that, because it was so stiff, it didn't move. But my right breast still had a lot of breast tissue, so when I walked or worked out it jiggled while the left one stayed put. It was pretty obvious to me and I didn't like it. I was definitely not going to keep them that way. Maybe the third time would be the charm.

While I was dealing with having my second reconstruction, Naomi, my client/co-worker who'd brought me meals while I was recovering from my mastectomy, was having a mastectomy on her left breast. She was in her mid-forties and had discovered from a routine mammogram that she had stage 0 breast cancer. However, when she'd opted to have a mastectomy and her doctor did the sentinel node biopsy she discovered it was in one of her lymph nodes. That put her at stage II. Naomi had really been through a tough time. Her father lost a long battle with prostate cancer a few months before her diagnosis. Shortly after her father passed Naomi went through a layoff and she lost her job.

A while back Diane, Naomi, and I had taken a trip to Santa Cruz and we visited a cute little shop that had lots of unique stationary, cards, and trinkets. I'd found a rock with *Bliss* painted on it, which I thought would be a good reminder of what I'm hoping to attain in my life based on that experience I'd had. I'd also seen a few cancer related books and cards. One card that I decided to buy had a poem called "What Cancer Cannot Do." I'd bought it so I'd have the poem printed out nicely somewhere. However, once Naomi was diagnosed with breast cancer I thought it would be nice to send to her. Who knew when I was buying that card that one of the people who was with me would receive it because they'd have cancer? I couldn't believe cancer was striking in my circle again.

I was at work a few months after my second surgery when one of my clients, Lisa, who I always saw but never really spoke to, struck up a conversation with me in the break room. I'd never found her to be approachable so we'd never talked.

She said, "Do you live around here?"

I said, "Yes, I live in Dublin not far from the office in a one bedroom apartment that is driving me and my husband crazy. I wish we could buy a larger condo or a house but the Bay Area is so pricey."

"You'd be surprised how many deals there are out there

since the economy has taken a dive. There are a lot of nice looking foreclosures on the market."

It turned out that Lisa moonlighted as a real estate agent, so she sent me some listings to give me an idea of what was on the market. I would have loved to own a home but with my student loan and all of the debt I'd accumulated I hadn't given home-ownership any serious thought. Prior to living in Paris I hadn't wanted to purchase a home because I didn't want to lay down roots anywhere. Now, I was married and we were ready to have more space and make an investment. The U.S. was sliding into a recession during the election and there were a lot of layoffs and foreclosures as a result. We decided to look in Stockton because it was less expensive. It was also the foreclosure capital of the U.S. We would have plenty of inventory to choose from. After what seemed like an eternity of looking, we found a cute home in a gated community in South Stockton. Once upon a time the house had gone for upwards of $300,000, but was now selling for $147,000. We got a steal. It needed very little work— just a good cleaning and some new carpet. But we could man-age with shampooing the carpet until we could afford to change it. Our mortgage turned out to be less than our rent for the squeezy one bedroom apartment in Dublin. Stockton is about an hour commute for me during work hours but having an asset and four times the square footage was worth it to me.

Shortly after we moved into our new house, Jamal received some great news from his attorney. The court had dismissed his embezzlement case! Since the arrest, his attorney was building a case and drawing the whole process out so that Jamal could be with me during treatment. Jamal had to serve time for the DUI which also pushed things out. The ninety days Jamal served for the DUI was nothing compared to the time he was facing with the embezzlement charge. Embezzlement was a felony and he was looking at up to twenty years.

His preliminary hearing in which a judge listened to the evidence on both sides to determine if there was probable cause to take the case to trial had been like a comedy of errors. The judge was old and hard of hearing. The only witness the defense had was the detective who had a personal vendetta against Jamal. She was chewing gum on the witness stand and she spoke softly or at least not loud enough for someone who is hard of hearing. When the attorneys questioned her, the judge kept asking her to turn toward him so that he could hear her. She would turn but then she'd slowly go back to facing forward. Every time she answered Jamal's attorney's questions the little old judge would say, "What did you say? I can't hear you. Can you turn toward me?" I thought for sure they needed to throw the case out. Not only because the judge probably hadn't heard anything that was being said, but also because Jamal's attorney was making the detective look like a fool. He basically proved that she hadn't taken the evidence and tried to find a suspect. Instead, she'd taken a suspect and tried to make the evidence fit him. She hadn't questioned or considered anyone else but Jamal. The judge ruled to let the case go to trial but shortly after that it kept changing prosecutors, I think because no one wanted to have a loss on their record. The evidence wasn't there to convict Jamal.

With Jamal's case dismissed and my treatment finished, and owning a new home, things were definitely looking up for us. I just needed to get my titty situation worked out. I was going to have another surgery. This time I'd live with whatever the results were. I went with silicone this time. The two saline implants I had were just too hard. I wanted something suppler and silicone is supposed to feel more like a real breast. Dr. Galani convinced me that silicone was safer now so I decided to go for it. We'd take out the two implants and go for one silicone implant and we'd take out some breast tissue in the right breast so it wouldn't jiggle so much and put a larger implant in that one.

Once I healed from that surgery I invited my girlfriends from Paris to visit since I had room to have guests. Cynthia flew in from Vancouver, B.C., Kay flew in from Toronto, and Caryn flew in from Dallas. I'm sure they were surprised to see how big I was. I'd gotten as big as two hundred and five pounds. So I did wind up gaining the dreaded twenty five pounds after chemo. I don't know if I could officially blame cancer since chemo had been so long ago, but I unofficially blamed it on cancer. Had my life gone on as usual I would never have let myself get that big. I wouldn't have been so adamant about the saying life is short, eat dessert first. I wouldn't have done so much emotional eating and I would have denied myself a little more. Before cancer I'd been well on my way to getting in shape. After, it was a struggle. I hated being that big! I was huge! I felt like a lot of my weight gain stemmed from all the different medications I was on. I had a fat stomach! I could thank Tamoxifen for that. I'd never had a fat stomach in my life. If anyone asked me if I was pregnant I was gonna scream! I could definitely notice the effect some of the medications had on my brain and emotions. Some of the drugs made you not want to eat. Some of them made you hungry all the time. I never was a nighttime snacker but since the drugs interrupted my sleep pattern I'd be up at night and want to munch on something. If I could have slept through the night I wouldn't have had a problem. I wouldn't have even known I was hungry until the morning. Being married was no help either. We liked to wine and dine, and when I pay to eat I don't like to be hungry afterward so no salads for me. I love to eat, drink, and be merry but I now needed to find some balance.

All three of the girls looked great and were physically fit and active. Seeing them was great inspiration for me. One thing was for sure—the spread I made for them the day they arrived wasn't going to get me where I wanted to be. I cooked a huge Mexican meal: chicken enchiladas, chile relleno casserole, beans and rice, margaritas, homemade salsa and guacamole, and Jamal made us two flavors of Jell-O shots. I'd originally thought about having fondue but we all agreed that we would keep that experience in Paris. It just wouldn't have been the same. After dinner we all sat on the couch and watched a French film. Something we all enjoyed but not many of my other friends did. Jamal looked down on us from upstairs as we watched the movie, amazed that there were others out there like me.

The next morning as we were getting dressed I decided to show the girls my new breasts. I was excited to show them off and they were anticipating seeing them because I'd been waiting to heal before they could visit. I opened my robe and explained to them that it was still a work in progress. Cynthia blurted out in her outspoken fashion, "They're lopsided!" I explained to her what Dr. Galani had explained to me after each surgery, which was that the right breast was swollen and would need to go down and also adding the nipple would help. She responded, "There's not that much swelling in the world. They're lopsided." Caryn and Kay didn't say much but I could tell they were shocked that Cynthia had had the audacity to say such things. There was no love lost though. I didn't take it personally. It's not like I'd done my own reconstruction. And I needed to get an honest opinion. I think sometimes people feel so sorry for you that they don't want to hurt your feelings. Cynthia doesn't have that filter. And she was right. They were still lopsided.

We finished getting dressed and headed to San Francisco. We hit the road in a cute little red Chevy HHR that I'd rented. It looks like a Chevy Suburban from the forties. We lovingly named it Big Red. We met some other classmates who happened to be in town at the Ferry Building and then we wandered into a nice Peruvian restaurant for lunch. After lunch, we walked around Fisherman's Wharf. Then we decided to tour San Fran by car. Next we continued on to San Jose and had dinner on Santana Row at a little French restaurant called the Left Bank. It was like a mini class reunion. Just like old times.

Napa was the plan for the following day. I'd chosen to take them to Sterling Vineyards. It's the only winery in Napa that you need to ride a gondola to get to because it's on a hill. I had purchased a bottle of Bitch wine a couple of years back that I'd been saving for a special occasion. Jamal wouldn't appreciate sharing a pink bottle of Bitch with me so a girlfriend reunion was the perfect occasion. We packed up some fruit, cheeses, smoked salmon, and other hors d'oeuvres and we had a little picnic on the grounds of the winery. Afterwards we toured the winery and tasted wines. The view from Sterling Vineyards is beautiful. You can see just about all of Napa. The wine was good too.

We crammed a lot into a three day weekend but it was a well-deserved trip for all of us. We'd missed each other and it had been three years since we'd been together. We put some miles on Big Red but we had a blast!

It was evident a few months out from my last reconstruction that I still wasn't getting the look I want so I decided not to go back to Dr. Galani to let him put the cherry on top if you know what I mean. This job wasn't finished. I decided to concentrate on getting my weight down and then try another doctor. I knew Dr. Galani had tried to spare me from having the dorsal flap surgery but I thought that was probably what I needed.

I saw a lady who was taking chemo at the same time as me and her breasts looked great from what I could tell. She told me that she was thrilled with her reconstruction and gave me her surgeon's number. She had a lot of nice things to say about him. So there were some people out there who were satisfied with their surgery. I just wasn't one of them yet.

Jamal's sister Toni came over to our house to visit. Her Miniature Schnauzer had had four puppies, two boys and two girls. They were the cutest things. You could hold them in the palm of your hand and they were just starting to open their eyes. Toni had to monitor them 24/7. She was starting to get a little cabin fever. So she came over with the puppies in tow. Jamal and I had discussed getting a dog but we realized that it was a lot of work. Also, I'm allergic to dog dander so I'd need a dog that's hypoallergenic. I'd been thinking about a Poodle or Labrador or a combination of the two. When we were holding Toni's puppies, she mentioned that the one I had wasn't taken yet and she'd give him to me if I wanted. She was pretty much giving them all away. One was going to the stud's owner. One was going to Toni's dog's breeder since her dog had died. She planned to sell only one of them to the stud's owner's friend. Toni asked me what I'd name him if I kept him. I took a long look at him with his black body, white paws, and the white that ran across his chest and I said, "He looks like he's wearing a tuxedo. I would name him Armani." Toni said, "Armani! That's a good name. Armani." Jamal and I talked it over and decided to pay her for the puppy. It was a lot of work to breed dogs. He was going to be my little Christmas gift but I wouldn't get him until the New Year since he needed to be eight weeks old before he could leave his mother.

Karla's Column

What Cancer Cannot Do
Author Unknown

Cancer is so limited...
It cannot cripple love.
It cannot shatter hope.
It cannot corrode faith.
It cannot eat away peace.
It cannot destroy confidence.
It cannot kill friendship.
It cannot shut out memories.
It cannot silence courage.
It cannot reduce eternal life.
It cannot quench the Spirit.

Survivorship: Year Three

CHAPTER FIFTEEN:
Giving and Receiving

"I am only one, but still I am one. I cannot do everything, but still I can do something; and because I cannot do everything, I will not refuse to do something that I can do."

--Helen Keller

*J*amal and I decided to ring in 2010 in Las Vegas. Jamal loves Las Vegas and had been longing to return ever since he'd left everything behind to marry me. I'd never been in Vegas on New Year's so I was excited. We were staying at the Orleans, which is off the strip but a little more quaint. It's Jamal's favorite hotel & casino and my cousin, Chris, happens to bartend there. He got us a great rate on the room.

The first day we were there I walked straight up to Chris at the bar and said, "Where is the hot spot? Where do people win?" He said, "Somebody wins up here at the bar every day. It's video poker progressive. You have to play the maximum bet."

Hitting the jackpot was my mission for the trip. I'd gone to Vegas and Reno before and I hated playing the slots because I never won. I didn't really know how to play video poker so Jamal was trying to show me a little later that evening but at that point I'd had one too many drinks and I was screwing up. Jamal and I were both frustrated and drunk and we were drawing attention to ourselves because we were talking so loud. I decided it was a good idea to hang up gambling for the night. You have to think to play video poker and my mind wasn't clear.

We were just hanging out at the bar when someone said, "There goes Joe Jackson!" as in Michael Jackson's dad. Chris said he hung out there a lot. I wanted to have my picture taken with him so I went up to him and introduced myself. I asked for a picture and he acted annoyed but I could tell he liked having a fan. We took a picture and I expressed my condolences for Michael Jackson's death. Michael Jackson had passed away that June from a bad reaction to some anesthetics that were administered to him. It was such a shocker. The world mourned him for weeks. In fact, Jamal and I had had an impromptu memorial celebration at our house the week that he passed. Toni, one of her girlfriends, and Toni's daughter came by. Toni had brought a Michael Jackson CD so we popped it into the CD player. A few margaritas later we were all in the kitchen in our socks moonwalking or trying to at least. We sang and danced all night. I even got on the computer to look up the lyrics to "Wanna Be Starting Something" so that I could sing the words properly. That is one song that I don't understand. You're a vegetable??? Ma ma se, ma ma sa, ma ma coo sa??? Nonetheless, Michael is and will always be the man and I was one degree away from him had he still been alive. I think Joe Jackson really made the Jackson kids sing. He probably did some things wrong but he did make them the professionals that they are today in my opinion. I thought it was pretty cool to meet him.

The next day I decided to cop a squat at the bar where I'd been the previous night and try my luck on video poker. I was only going to drink ginger ale this time. I wanted to have a clear mind. The minimum bet on the machine was a quarter and the max bet was seventy five cents. I decided if nothing else I would sit and have fun. If the machine let me play with the money I'd budgeted I'd keep playing, even if I was just breaking even. I was just going to enjoy it and not be uptight. I won a few hands. I thought the machine really liked me. Jamal played on a different game behind me. After about thirty minutes of sitting there and getting a few straights and flushes, I hit the jackpot. A royal flush! The machine blinked "Call Attendant." The jackpot was a little over $1,000. Jamal was so excited and so was I. An attendant came over and paid me in cold hard cash. That was New Year's Eve. What a way to start the party off! Later that night we went down to the Strip so that we could see the fireworks and be in the mix. We both thought it was a little overrated but I felt it was one of those things that you have to experience if you're in Vegas on New Year's or you'll always wish you had. It was cold and crowded and it was hard to get a taxi to get us back to our hotel. Next time if we are there again for New Year's I'd be content to stay in the hotel and watch the fireworks from the room.

The next day since I had a little cash I thought I'd gamble a little more. I liked gambling sober. Maybe that was my good luck charm. I got myself a latte and sat down at a nickel machine called Ten Times Pay. There was a symbol that, if you landed on it, would pay you ten times the amount you'd normally win. It wasn't long that I was on that machine before it paid me 5,000 nickels. That's $250! I'd always hated playing on the under one dollar slots because I would get all excited when I won, only to learn it was about ten dollars or something small. But the dollar machines can take your money fast and unless I get lucky fast I really don't have money to blow like that. That's why I was on the nickel machine. This time it was paying me enough money to write home about.

I texted Jamal, who was over on the craps table, and told him I'd won. He left the craps table and advised me to pull my winnings out and put fifty dollars back in and play that. That way I wouldn't give it all back. So I did. Wouldn't you know, a few spins later the machine paid me 10,000 nickels. Five hundred dollars! Jamal came over and was amazed. He told me to do the same thing. Pull out the winnings and put fifty dollars back in and play. There was a lady next to me who was so frustrated that I was winning and she wasn't. She had played my machine and hadn't had any luck so she'd moved to the next machine over. You should have seen her slamming those buttons and cussing. I thought *This machine likes me*. I put my little winnings away and played my little fifty dollars and as God is my witness I hit the jackpot! Twenty-five thousand nickels! One thousand two hundred fifty dollars!

I had hit a jackpot on New Year's Eve and one on New Year's Day. The first day of 2010 I hit the jackpot that pays ten times the money. I thought that was pretty funny. I'd never been particularly lucky but maybe my luck was beginning to change. Very encouraging after the last few years I'd had. With all my winnings, Jamal and I had so much fun gambling and not feeling restricted by budget. He taught me how to play roulette and we had bets sprawled across the table. Those two jackpots kicked up the fun factor. It was nice that he no longer had a gambling problem.

We returned from Vegas and shortly after we picked up Armani. Toni had him dressed in a cute little scarf. We had a small crate for him and a toy. He whimpered a little on the ride home and when we put him down on the floor of the house he looked so sad. I'm sure he missed his mom and siblings. He warmed up to us pretty quickly though and really took to me. He's my little shadow. I've never had my own dog before and I don't have kids so it's amazing to me how much Armani loves me. I can't go anywhere without him following me. He's so affectionate and sweet. He loves to cuddle and be close. Jamal would feed him and play with him but I was the one he liked to spend his time with. He's the cutest little thing.

It's nice that Toni was his breeder because she'd dog sit for us. It worked out because Armani got to see his mother, although I don't think he cares that she's his mom. He constantly tried to hump her.

Jamal and I planned to go to Washington D.C. for St. Patrick's Day. I finally used those flight vouchers I'd received when I got bumped on my way to Dallas to visit my sister. I booked the flights just before the vouchers expired. There weren't many places that we could go. They only allot a few seats on every flight for vouchers. The popular destinations like Miami and New York were booked for every date I chose so I thought, *Why not go to Washington D.C.?* I'd never been there. It was always someplace I wanted to see but if I'd had to pay I probably would have gone to other places first. I'd really wanted to attend President Obama's Inauguration but it had been too difficult finding hotels and it really wasn't feasible so I had to watch from my living room. I'd heard that St. Patrick's Day is a festive time to be in D.C. I'd seen the St. Patrick's Day Parade on

TV and had heard that they dye the fountain at the White House green. And depending on how Mother Nature felt, there would possibly even be some cherry blossoms.

Several months prior to our departure, I contacted my Congressman's office, Dennis Cardoza, to arrange a White House tour for us. One of his staff assistants whose name was Katharine said she'd let us know about a week or two before we were scheduled to arrive if we were able to make the list. She was going to arrange some other tours for us as well. She took all of our personal information for the background check (everyone who visits the White House has to have one) and I crossed my fingers that there would be room for us on the White House tour list. I was also crossing my fingers that President Obama would be in town. He was scheduled to go to Asia the week of St. Patrick's Day. Possibly being able to spot the president would make my trip much more exciting.

As the trip drew closer we considered not going because Jamal was concerned about the weather. It had snowed a week or two prior to our trip and it was possible that it would snow again. We also didn't know if we could really afford the trip. Like so many other Americans at that time, Jamal had been laid off from his job. Thankfully he was able to get unemployment but we still were tight for money. It seemed better financially to just let the tickets go to waste. However, when we received our White House tour confirmation, I thought we'd be passing up a great opportunity. Katharine had arranged for us to sit in on the House and Senate sessions as well. I really wanted to go and Jamal could see that I wasn't really going to take no for an answer or that if we didn't go he'd never hear the end of it. So he acquiesced. We'd really have to do it on a budget.

I was hoping and praying that President Obama would cancel his trip even though I thought that was highly unlikely. But it doesn't hurt to ask. One morning as I was getting dressed for work I heard on the news that health care reform was back on the House's agenda. This would be the final opportunity to get it passed. Since President Obama had taken office there hadn't been much progress made regarding health care. It seemed they couldn't get the bill just right and therefore didn't have enough votes in support of it. After a few months of back and forth between the Democrats and Republicans, I'd started to tune out. I'd get emails from Organizing for America (OFA), formerly Obama for America, but for some reason I just wasn't getting out there and getting involved. Hearing that this was our final effort was probably the push I needed. I snapped out of my inertia and started looking at ways I could get involved during my vacation.

Although providing health care for all Americans sounds like a no brainer, the Republicans, and this new party offshoot called the Tea Party, were vehemently opposed to health care reform. They called President Obama a socialist, a Nazi, and anything else they could think of. For a party that wears their religion on their sleeves the GOP sure does lack compassion. They didn't care that some people who get cancer or other life threatening illnesses couldn't get health care coverage or if they had coverage were suddenly dropped when they needed coverage most. Emotions ran high on this topic so I knew we were in for a fight.

I kept checking BarackObama.com to see what volunteer opportunities were available in the D.C. area. An event showed up about a few days before we were scheduled to leave. Organizing for America headquarters was holding a phone bank on the Thursday before the House vote, which was scheduled for Sunday. I signed up to make calls and within days my prayer was answered. President Obama decided to cancel his trip to Asia. He had cancelled other trips with the hope of getting health care reform passed but I knew this time would be different. I was excited that I'd be in D.C. during such a historic time.

Jamal's cousin works for the Marriott and let us use his friends and family discount. However, none of the hotels were in D.C. proper. They were all a good distance away and we'd need a rental car. I was having a hard time deciding between staying in Maryland or Virginia but I decided on Chantilly, VA at the last minute. I had actually booked Maryland and then changed it to Chantilly. It wasn't ideal not being in D.C. but I would make-do. I was no stranger to driving long distances being that I live in Stockton and commute to the Bay Area—a forty minute drive that can turn into an hour and a half ride during peak travel time.

We arrived in D.C. the day before St. Patrick's Day and we decided to spend it in Arlington. We had no idea what was going on in the town but Jamal saw this pub on the news that had outdoor tents, live music, and looked like it was really preparing for a big celebration so we decided to go there. It was called Ireland's Four Courts. We had a good time but we could tell that some people were wondering what our black asses were doing there. In fact, an older white lady who was there with her husband leaned over to Jamal and said, "You don't look Irish." and she didn't say it with a smile on her face. Jamal laughed at her and said, "We're the O'Mitchells." She didn't think it was too funny but we both thought it was. There's something about Virginia and other former slave states. There's a little residual racism in those places. You can just feel it in the air. Virginia is a nice place to visit but I wouldn't want to live there.

The next morning I got a posting on Facebook from the White House that read, "In the D.C. area? Don't miss this event with President Obama tomorrow." The president was going to hold his last health care rally at George Mason University, which was right down the street from our hotel. I couldn't believe it. Booking the hotel in Chantilly had been a good idea. If I'd stayed in Maryland I wouldn't have gotten up at the wee hours of the morning to travel such a distance to make it to the rally in time. Now I was super excited. I'd volunteer that day and the next day I'd see the president get everyone pumped up to get health care reform passed.

I dropped Jamal off at ESPN Zone on the way to volunteer. It was March Madness, which is how I kept Jamal content while I volunteered. I went to the Democratic National Headquarters where Organizing for America is also headquartered, not far from the Capitol. We were making calls to the constituents of members of Congress who were undecided on health care reform. I was calling Representative Susan Kosmas' constituents asking them to call her office to ask her to vote yes for health care reform. There were about ten to fifteen of us making calls. One of the OFA volunteers who organizes the phone banks asked if I could come back on Saturday and make more calls. I told her I had my White House tour that day but I'd check with my husband and see if he didn't mind me coming afterwards. They knew I was on vacation. People found it hard to believe that I hadn't planned to be there for health care reform. I explained to them that I'd planned my trip months before I knew health care reform was back on the agenda. It just worked out that I was able to VolunTour (volunteer + tourism). I'd heard that is a new term people are using when they mix vacation and charity work. More and more people are interested in giving back on their vacations. I'd wanted to VolunTour and had thought I'd go somewhere like New Orleans, but my first VolunTour trip happened to be D.C. Just because I was VolunTouring, I didn't want

Jamal to think our whole trip would be about me making phone calls. However, he was understanding because he could just go back to ESPN Zone and watch more basketball. Give him a beer and television and he's fine. He also knew being there meant a lot to me and he could sense my enthusiasm.

The next morning I got up around six a.m. so that I could be at the health care rally early and hopefully get a seat on the floor. There weren't as many protesters outside the rally as I'd anticipated. There were about fifty of them by the time the doors to the gymnasium opened. They were stationed right across from the line to go inside. They had a lot of crazy signs like *ObamaCare Will Kill Us*! and *Hands Off My Health Care!* and *Kill the Bill!* There were people passing out pocket-size books of the Constitution. I guess they wanted to educate us on how unconstitutional it was to provide health care to everyone. At one point the group of them assembled together to say the Pledge of Allegiance as if demons were going to flee us once they recited it. There was one guy with a loud speaker who was ranting about why "ObamaCare," as they called it, wasn't good. He said, "Health care reform will cost us $40,000 per person!" I shouted back, "I've got more than that in student loans!" Everyone in line laughed and he looked stunned and embarrassed. You can't scare me with $40,000 of debt.

I managed to get a fairly decent seat. To my dismay I'd have never had a seat on the floor no matter how early I'd gotten there. Those were reserved for people who had tickets. Nonetheless my seat was pretty good. I was thrilled to finally be at a rally, especially at such a historic time, and to finally see the president in person. Every time he was in California I'd missed him. Early on in his campaign I'd been in the throes of my battle with cancer so I couldn't go then. One time I was in Reno and he was due in town the day after I left. I couldn't seem to coordinate making it to a rally.

The president graced the stage with his usual swagger, took off his jacket, rolled up his sleeves, and gave a rousing speech on why now was the time for health care reform. He laid to rest all of the rumors about how health care reform was going to create death panels for the elderly and how government was taking over health care. This was the moment! You could definitely feel it in the air. He was going to get health care reform done.

I left that auditorium feeling inspired. I'd just witnessed a part of history. For some reason I walked to the opposite side of the building from where my car was parked. I heard the roaring of a motorcycle engine and then sirens. It was the president's motorcade. His custom made armored Cadillac limousine, dubbed The Beast, floated by with its U.S. and presidential flags waving in the wind. There were actually three presidential limos so that you wouldn't be able to tell which one he was in. An ambulance trailed behind, which is a customary part of the motorcade. Everyone was cheering as the motorcade sped by.

I dashed back to the hotel after the rally to pick up Jamal who had slept in. His idea of a vacation is not getting up at six in the morning. We headed to the Capitol to pay a visit to Representative Cardoza. His office was holding tickets for us to sit in on the health care reform vote on Sunday. We also wanted to meet Representative Cardoza and tell him that we wanted him to vote yes on health care reform. He's a Blue Dog Democrat. Blue Dog Democrats are a group of fiscally conservative Democrats. Several of the Blue Dogs were undecided on health care reform because of the costs. I wanted to make sure that my congressman heard from me, his constituent.

Representative Cardoza's office is in the Longworth Building of the Congressional Office Buildings. When we arrived we went through a metal detector but then were simply allowed to enter the building and go wherever we pleased. No one asked us who we were there to see or anything. I found that very strange and pretty disturbing in light of all the tension that was mounting in regard to health care reform. Jamal and I walked the halls taking note of the brass name plates to the side of the doors. We thought it was pretty cool that we were seeing the offices of politicians we'd watched on the news.

We entered Dennis Cardoza's office, which had pictures of him with other notable politicians including President Obama. There was a television in his waiting area tuned in to C-Span so his aides and visitors could know what was going on when the House was in session. Katharine greeted us and gave us our tickets for the House Gallery.

"Thank you so much for coordinating all of this Katharine. I really appreciate it." I said.

"No problem."

"Is Representative Cardoza available? I want to get a picture with him. Also I'm a breast cancer survivor and I'd like to ask him to vote yes on health care reform."

"Unfortunately the House is in session so he's not in." She gestured toward the TV and the live broadcast of the House floor. "I can take your picture in his office though if you'd like and I'll leave him a note letting him know that you're in favor of health care reform."

I thought that having a picture in Representative Cardoza's office would be a pretty cool consolation prize for not getting to meet him so Jamal and I sat down in the two big leather library chairs in his office and posed for a couple of pictures. I made a joke when I posted them on Facebook that our representative thought we were so cool that he took *our* picture instead of us taking his.

After we left Representative Cardoza's office, Jamal and I walked around the Capitol and then headed to our hotel. I uploaded our pictures from the day onto my laptop when I got to our room and noticed that the photo of us in Representative Cardoza's office included his dry erase board with a tally of how his constituents weighed in on health care reform. He had a list of pros and cons and reasons constituents were or were not in support of the bill. The pros significantly outweighed the cons.

I wasn't sure if we should have been privy to such information since Representative Cardoza hadn't publicly stated how he was going to vote. However, if he voted the way his constituents wanted him to, his vote was going to be "yes" on Sunday. All that was on the news was which representatives were still undecided and the media was speculating about how they would vote. I had a scoop! I quickly logged into my CNN iReport account, which I hadn't used since New Year's Eve 2008 and posted the picture with the headline "CA Rep. Dennis Cardoza has more Pros than Cons on Health Care Reform Bill." I was hoping Katharine wouldn't get in trouble for letting us take the picture.

In the morning we went to D.C. for our long awaited White House tour. It was hot and humid and naturally I was sweating like a pig and was the only one who was doing so. Ugh! How annoying! Another slight disappointment was that the White House tour was a lot shorter than I thought it would be and the White House was also a lot smaller. The Blue Room, Red Room, Green Room, and East Room are all very close together. However, every room is so meticulously and opulently decorated. I loved it! It reminded me of being in the Versailles Palace. Beautiful, glistening chandeliers, rich fabrics, perfectly arranged flowers, and valuable paintings. Except instead of the paintings being French royalty they are of past presidents and first ladies. The East Room was my favorite with its yellow color scheme. I liked it because I'd seen the president make speeches in there and I'd seen pictures of dinner parties that had taken place in that room. It was the room where the fun takes place.

After our tour, which lasted less than thirty minutes, we walked around to the north side of the White House to take pictures. There was a huge protest going on. The streets were filled with people. Police motorcycles lined the streets and there was an armored paddy wagon. There were people handing out fliers and someone was speaking over a loud speaker on Lafayette Square, the park just in front of the White House. There were people in a circle beating drums, an Uncle Sam character on stilts, even clowns, and all kinds of other eccentric demonstrators. I thought I was in a hippie time warp. One older guy was wearing what looked like a house dress and was dancing to the drums in some sort of a daze and chanting, "We're gonna end this war" while he waved around a picket sign that read, *Indict Bush* I later found out that that day was the seventh anniversary of the start of the War in Iraq. Protesters were there to hold President Obama's feet to the fire for the promise he'd made to end the war.

Jamal and I walked around to check out the happenings. I noticed snipers walking across the roof of the White House, which was pretty cool and scary at the same time. I hear they are there all the time but I'm sure they were on high alert with all of the protests and demonstrations that were taking place. We took some pictures in front of the White House and then I headed to the OFA headquarters to make more phone calls.

It was the day before the vote. We made calls from a different room this time. We had a lot more volunteers and needed more space and phones. We called several different representatives' constituents. The energy level was high. After about a half hour of calling, we heard the news that one of the representatives we were making calls for had decided to vote yes. There was a series of cheers and high fives and we checked that person off of our list and called the next representatives' constituents. We were told so many people were calling their representatives that their D.C. office lines and local office lines were busy. Shortly after one of the victory announcements my phone rang. I could tell from the caller ID that it was someone in the D.C. area. I answered the phone.

"Mrs. Mitchell?" said the caller.

"Yes?" I said trying to hear over all the cheering and celebrating.

"Hi. It's Katharine. I just wanted to call and let you know that Representative Cardoza has decided to vote yes tomorrow."

"Oh that's great Katharine! Thank you so much for calling!"

"You're welcome. I know it means a lot to you."

"Yes, it does."

"Well take care and enjoy your House visit tomorrow."

"I will. Thank you so much!"

I was so excited and couldn't believe that Katharine had taken the time to call little old me to let me know the news. I was feeling influential and powerful. I could tell that we were on the cusp of getting health care reform passed. Victory was in the air.

I was so excited to go back to the Capitol the next day that I decided to go to Target and get supplies to make a sign to show my support for the bill. I was seeing too many Tea Partiers on the news with their *Kill the Bill!* and *Don't Tread on Me!* signs. I wanted to make sure the news saw the other side of the debate. I'd also heard on the news that Tea Party protesters had gone to the Longworth Building Saturday afternoon and called Representative John Lewis, a veteran of the Civil Rights Movement, a "nigger," and Representative Barney Frank, one of the first openly gay representatives, a "faggot." Representative Emmanuel Cleaver, another African American, said that he was spat upon by one of the protesters. Representative Louise Slaughter had had a brick thrown through the window of her Buffalo, NY office. No one was injured thankfully. I wasn't surprised to hear about what had happened in the Longworth Building. I'd felt security wasn't high enough there.

Sunday afternoon I headed down to the Capitol with my sign that read, *I'M A CANCER SURVIVOR AND I'M PRO LIFE… MINE. "YES" TO HEALTH CARE INSURANCE REFORM.* One of the Right Wings' ill-informed arguments against supporting health care reform was that it would use federal money to fund abortions, as if everyone who wanted an abortion could just waltz into a clinic, no questions asked. The health care bill would support abortions in the case of rape or incest but I guess the GOP would like women to keep their "little inbred babies" who wouldn't have health care once they were born. My thought was, a life is a life. You've got an unborn child on one hand and a taxpaying, productive citizen with cancer on the other. Which is more important? Who's to say? I knew my sign would get under those supposed pro-lifers' skin.

When we walked up to the Capitol, I could hear cheering and booing but I couldn't see what was going on because the sounds were coming from the hilly side of the Capitol. As I got closer, holding my sign proudly, I saw barricades and officers. I asked one of the officers if I could get closer to see what was going on. He told me that I could go wherever I wanted. I had just passed a group of people in support of health care reform but none of them seemed to want to get closer to the crowd facing the Capitol balcony. It seemed they were a little scared. I wanted to see what was going on and, since the officer had said I could go down there, I did. The commotion was caused by some of the representatives, both Democrats and Republicans, that were coming out on the balcony of the Capitol waving to the crowd. I didn't get into the thick of the crowd because once I got to the outskirts I realized the people didn't look like my kind. They were mean looking. Something had them pissed off. There was a sea of anti-health care signs, *Stop Government Takeover!* and *What part of NO don't you understand?!* and there were tons of American flags. A symbol of one of the Right Wings' insinuations—that they're more patriotic than Democrats. They acted as if they thought they were more American too. I stood on a ledge next to some Tea Partiers and looked toward the balcony. I noticed Barney Frank on one level and GOP Representative John Boehner on another level. But I wasn't standing on that ledge even one minute before this hillbilly looking man yelled, "Baby killer!" at me. As soon as he started in on me this woman who looked like she didn't have dental coverage walked up to me and said, "You don't belong over here." She was evil! I didn't know if she was racist or crazy but I asked her what she meant by telling me I didn't belong there. I told her the police officer told me that I could go wherever I wanted. She said, "This is the Tea Party area!" I think she was possessed by the devil she was so mad at me. I was dividing my attention between her and the hillbilly and asking him why he thought I was a baby killer just because I'm pro my own life. He was yelling back at me, speaking so passionately that he was spitting, which I think he was doing on purpose. Someone yelled out, "Get a job!" as if I didn't have one.

Jamal was getting pissed off because the hillbilly was getting too close to me. He'd warned me not to go down to the area because he thought he'd have to hurt somebody if they got out of line. He'd been right. It hadn't been a good idea. I didn't want a riot to start. That could have changed the whole trajectory of health care reform so we left to avoid a physical altercation. We walked back to the pro-health care reform area with me proudly holding my sign to make sure the crazies saw it. People in support of health care reform let me know that they loved my sign. One guy approached me from a German TV station to ask me why I was at the Capitol and while he was interviewing me a Japanese reporter came up and asked me a few questions and took notes too. The German reporter asked if he could film so I did an on camera interview with him. Jamal and I stood inside the barricade that lined the representatives' path from the House Office Buildings to the Capitol Building. I was waving my sign and yelling "Health Care Now!" when representative John Lewis walked by. Jamal was thrilled to shake his hand as he made his way to the Capitol.

We decided that we shouldn't spend too much time outside or we might miss the vote so we headed over to the House Gallery entrance. The line was long. Every visitor was only allowed to sit in for fifteen minutes so that everyone would get a chance to visit. You could get in line as many times as you wanted though. I learned that passing a bill is a long process. They were first having a vote on the rules of the voting. That's the part we were able to witness. It was like a who's who for me and Jamal.

After our fifteen minutes were up, Jamal and I grabbed a bite to eat and a few beers at one of the pubs nearby while getting updates from passersby and the TV at the pub. It was getting dark and still no health care vote. I was willing to stay down at the Capitol until the official vote took place but as time went on it didn't look like it was going to happen until late that evening. Jamal was ready to leave and told me that it could be close to midnight before they got a vote. He thought it was stupid for us to wait and then have to drive back to Chantilly so we left. It turned out that he was right again. We watched the vote on C-Span from the comforts of our hotel and it didn't take place until after ten o' clock. The bill passed 219 to 212 with every Republican voting no. We'd done it! I was elated but I was also so exhausted that I fell asleep before President Obama could give his victory speech.

I woke up Monday with a hit list of sights to see. I didn't get to do a lot of sightseeing because I was VolunTouring and wrapped up in politics. I did manage to do a drive by of the Lincoln Memorial and Washington Monument but didn't see them up close. That day I was planning to actually tour the Capitol Building and visit the Smithsonian. In order to take my Capitol Building tour I had to have Katharine schedule it and escort me over so I went back to the Longworth Building. Katharine and I made a little small talk about the passing of the health care bill on the way over to the Capitol. She remarked that she'd been surfing the web and saw my iReport. She told me that she said, "That's Mrs. Mitchell!" I was shocked. It had only gotten fifty hits. I was surprised she'd even found it. She said that staying abreast on news circulating about Representative Cardoza was part of her job. I let her know that I'd been hoping she wouldn't get in trouble and she said she hadn't. She thought it was cool. She guided me to the Capitol Building via the underground tunnel and showed me where I'd start the tour. She really helped make my trip special. I thanked her for everything she'd done and we parted ways.

The next morning the president was scheduled to sign the Obama Health Care Bill into law and we were preparing to leave. I packed as I watched the signing ceremony feeling proud of what I'd helped achieve. I was feeling as if I had come to town just for the health care bill and my mission had been accomplished. I've witnessed the birth of a few of my friends' babies and health care reform felt similar. It had been the final push to birth health care reform and I'd been right there as a midwife. There were many people who'd made it happen but for some reason fate had made all of the pieces come together so that I could witness it from the front lines. I'm not sure why but perhaps this health care reform bill (now the Affordable Care Act) would mean more to me than I realized right then. It had been a memorable trip. Even Jamal had to admit it was good that we hadn't cancelled it.

Karla's Column

Armani's First Minutes at Home | Stockton, CA

Karla & Jamal in Rep. Cardoza's Office | Washington, D.C.

Karla Demonstrating in Support of Health Care Reform |
Washington, D.C.

CHAPTER SIXTEEN:
Baby, Baby, Please

*"She stood in the storm,
and when the wind did not blow her away,
she adjusted her sails."*

–Elizabeth Edwards

I was scheduled to have a PET scan in July. We flew my dad to town for his birthday. He and my mom had separated again. They were perpetually on again, off again. This time my mom packed up and moved to Dallas. All of my sisters were in Texas now and my dad was left in Seattle alone. His birthday was coming and I didn't want him to spend it by himself. Since he was in town I took him to my PET scan. It was nice having the moral support. It's always a little nerve-wracking to have a PET scan after you've had cancer. I'd been feeling little pains here and there from time to time and you just never know. I'd felt like I was the picture of health when I'd been diagnosed and look what had happened.

I had the PET scan done on a Friday and it usually takes

twenty-four to forty-eight hours to get the results. But since it was Friday I'd have to wait until Monday. On Monday Dr. Scott was off so I had to wait another day. I was on pins and needles as you can imagine but everything came back clear. I was glad because I was nearing the end of negotiations with PepsiCo. They'd approached me about coming aboard and I didn't want to have to decline because of my cancer recurring. I know it sounds like I expected the worst but I was just considering all the possible scenarios. I wouldn't be able to take a new job and switch insurance if I had to go through treatment again. Luckily, I was still NED so I didn't have to worry about that. A few weeks later I accepted the job. I'm not making six figures yet but it was a promotion for me and I'd have advancement potential, which was limited at my other job.

The other great thing was that PepsiCo had full knowledge of my medical history. I'd interviewed with a few other companies and I always worried about when to broach the subject about health care insurance and pre-existing conditions. I didn't want to receive a job offer and then have to spring my medical history on them. It seemed like revealing a weakness. Fortunately, PepsiCo knew all about my cancer history and still wanted to hire me, and their insurance policy covered pre-existing conditions so I'd be fine in that department.

I started my new job during the month I'd been waiting for—August. August marked two years that I'd been on Tamoxifen. I could start weaning myself off of it in hopes of having a baby. I'd been looking forward to this time but when August finally came and I spoke to Dr. Scott she sounded a little reluctant to have me stop taking it. I think she must have been talking with some of her colleagues and was now thinking that, with the number of lymph nodes that had been involved, she really wanted me to wait five years from my diagnosis before I tried to have a baby. That would be 2012 and I would be thirty-nine. Pushing forty and pushing a carriage was not my idea of a good time. She was more concerned that my risk of recurrence was highest in the first three years after treatment. She didn't want me to have a baby and then have something happen to me. I was of the mindset that if it was meant to be it would be. No one knows when they'll die. Someone perfectly healthy could have a baby today and then get hit by a bus tomorrow. I didn't want to live my life in fear—planning the future based on the worst that could happen. Of course, the decision was mine so I decided to stop taking my medicine.

Shortly after I stopped taking my medicine I felt a pain in my hip. It felt kind of like a muscle pain but I'd never had a pain there before. I told Dr. Scott about it and she suggested that I have another PET scan. She just wanted to make sure everything was okay before I got pregnant. I didn't want to have another PET scan. It had been nerve-wracking enough to have the last one. Plus, I'd decided to have a baby and I didn't want anything getting in the way. How could something change that fast? I'd just had a PET scan.

Weeks went by and the imaging clinic kept calling me to schedule the appointment and I kept ignoring them. I just continued to wean off my medication and was waiting for November to roll around, which would be when all of it would be out of my system and I could try to get pregnant. November came and although Jamal wanted a baby he was too tired to make love after work. He'd gotten a new job and was working six days a week, over sixty hours a week. It was challenging to come together during my ovulation window of opportunity.

Meanwhile, any little ache or pain I felt made me nervous. If Dr. Scott thought I needed to have another PET scan that meant she thought my cancer could come back that fast after the last PET scan. I started to freak out so I had a talk with Jamal about waiting three more years. He'd said that he wanted a baby. This wasn't solely my idea. But, at the rate we were going, we wouldn't conceive for several months and I couldn't just be off my medication indefinitely. We agreed to wait and if we couldn't have a biological child maybe we'd adopt. We were okay with that.

Since I was no longer planning to have a baby, I got back on Tamoxifen and decided to go ahead and have the second PET scan. I spoke with my mom and she encouraged me, that it was better to be safe than sorry and I agreed. This time I had my PET scan on a Monday. I wasn't really worried about the results but I was anxious to know what the test revealed. The pain in my hip had started to go away because I'd started to work out more. I thought it was arthritis or some sort of fluid buildup since I'd had my lymph nodes removed on the same side as the pain. The next day I decided to call Dr. Scott's office to let them know to contact me when they got the results and that's when I got nervous. I left a message on their recorder but as the minutes became hours it started to make me nervous. Maybe they hadn't called because Dr. Scott needed to speak to me herself because there was something wrong.

I got myself so worked up that I had to call my sister, Teressa, to comfort me. I told her I really didn't think anything was wrong but I'd called and left a message and now I was freaking out. We talked for a moment and just as we were getting off the phone she said, "Oh no! She died?" I said, "Who?" She said, "Elizabeth Edwards." Elizabeth Edwards was the wife of Senator John Edwards former 2008 presidential candidate. She'd been diagnosed with breast cancer in 2004 and it had recurred three years later during the 2008 campaign. She'd really used her platform to speak in support of health care reform. The news of her death was shocking because they'd just announced the week before that further treatment of her cancer would be futile but no one expected her to die so quickly after that news. She didn't look like she was near death. My mind started to race to the fact that her cancer had recurred three years after diagnosis and I was three years from my diagnosis. People try to act like that's the wrong way to think but it's a reality for many women. People are still dying of breast cancer.

I got off the phone with my sister after us both saying how sad it was about Elizabeth Edwards. Not even five minutes later Dr. Scott's office called to say I was still NED. "Oh, thank God!" I blurted out to the nurse on the line. "I just heard that Elizabeth Edwards died. I hadn't heard from you guys so I thought something was wrong. Thank you so much!" The nurse probably thought it was strange for me to be sharing all of that with her but who cares. I had to let it out. I was happy to be clear.

In 2007, my life was in disarray. I didn't know what the future held or even if I would be in it. But three years had passed and things were different. I was no longer mad at God, I had a beautiful home instead of a matchbox apartment, I had a better job, I was a pet parent to a beautiful Miniature Schnauzer, my hair was down to my shoulders, and Jamal was past his legal issues. My marriage? It still needed some work but thankfully we weren't dealing with as many challenges as we were three years ago. My life had changed quite a bit but the most important change was that I was cancer-free. I didn't have my D cups yet. I thought I'd wait until I was at my goal weight. I had about sixty pounds to lose and this was my year to do it. I turned my home office into a home office/home gym. I called it the TCB (Taking Care of Business) Room because it was where I "took care of business." I had an elliptical machine in there along with a Gold's Gym Home Gym. And remember my September issue of *Vogue*? Well it was also in the TCB Room. Turns out *Vogue* made its first ever documentary on producing the September issue and it happened to be about my 2007 issue. Now my free magazine is being offered on EBay for as much as $500!

My mind's eye was fully operating. I could visualize the future again. I saw myself having a fabulous party in 2013 when I'd not only have been cancer-free for five years but I would turn forty. The theme would be "FORTY, (cancer) FREE, and FABULOUS!" I only had two more years to go.

Survivorship: Year Four

CHAPTER SEVENTEEN:
Awareness

*"Second chances don't always mean a happy
ending. Sometimes it's just another shot to end
things right."*

--Unknown

*Y*ear three of my survivorship ended pretty uneventfully
and rolled into year four without fanfare. I was settling
into my new job and my new normal, which consisted of hot
flashes, sweating profusely, occasional joint and bone pain, and
continuing to see my doctor for quarterly visits. I hated taking
all of the drugs. Tamoxifen to prevent the cancer from returning, Effexor to help with the hot flashes caused by Tamoxifen,
and Warfarin to prevent blood clots since my family was prone
to them (and Tamoxifen also causes them). But I was alive and
I never missed an opportunity to tell people about my experience. So when my job chose me to be one of the employee
breast cancer survivors who would be featured on one of their
products for breast cancer awareness month, I was honored and

thrilled. I'd be one of three ladies gracing bottles of Gatorade that would be sold at Kroger stores nationwide during Kroger's "Giving Hope a Hand" breast cancer awareness campaign.

I applied on a Friday at the end of May and the next Monday I received the good news that I'd been accepted. The photo shoot would take place in New York City in the following two weeks. In the meantime, I tried to figure out how I could get Serena William's body in under fourteen days. I had all of the equipment at home but when I was eating right I wasn't working out. When I was working out, I wasn't eating right. The marketing team didn't ask me what kind of shape I was in so I guessed it wasn't important. Thank God, since I still hadn't lost the weight.

Two weeks passed quickly and I was whisked off to New York as a model of sorts. When I arrived at the studio there were several Kroger employee breast cancer survivors in the waiting area. They were being shot for store signage and the "Giving Hope a Hand" website. The two other PepsiCo employees and I were introduced to a representative from the ad agency who was organizing the photo shoot. She was showing us around the studio when I noticed that Mark Sanchez, Quarterback for the New York Jets, was being photographed. I also learned that Eli Manning, Quarterback for the New York Giants, was in the studio and being photographed as well. What a surprise! No one had mentioned that NFL players would be there. I saw that the Kroger ladies were being photographed with Mark and Eli and having pink Gatorade towels signed so I asked if the PepsiCo employees would get the opportunity to meet them as well. I was privileged enough just to be photographed and be on Gatorade bottles, but I was hoping we would have as much fun as the Kroger ladies. Either way this was an opportunity of a lifetime. How many people get the opportunity to be on a Gatorade bottle?

My PepsiCo colleagues and I stood around while everyone figured out what to do with us. There was a full team of people at the photo shoot—a hair and makeup team (or our Glam Squad as I like to call them), a stylist who would make sure our outfits were just so, an artistic director who would make sure we looked picture perfect, and photographer who had her own team of people to take care of lighting and proofing. While we were filling out release paperwork we learned that we would in fact be taking pictures with Eli Manning. I was so excited! This was so surreal and unexpected! At that point I thought we would just get pictures as mementos but right before my photo a lady from marketing came over to me and showed me a mockup of the Gatorade label. There was my name, a cartoon drawing of a stand in for me and Eli Manning. The two other PepsiCo employees and I would each be on a label with Eli! How exciting! This was the first year that the NFL's Breast Cancer Campaign, "A Crucial Catch," had teamed up with "Giving Hope a Hand" and the "Gatorade Breast Cancer Awareness" packaging. The addition of Eli would really heighten awareness, increase excitement, and sell a lot of Gatorade bottles for a great cause.

We did three different poses for the bottles and a video interview about our cancer experience for the website. It was great connecting with other survivors. As usual, they were all much older than me but we had our cancer experiences in common. It's always encouraging to talk to people who have gone through what you have and survived. I was so grateful to have had such a fabulous experience.

Shortly after I returned, I decided that I'd train to run the Susan G Komen 5K in San Francisco. I've never been a runner but I've always admired people who were. They always looked so cool and runner chicks always had great legs. Most everyone at my job was a runner and I thought a 5K would be a good starting race. Cynthia, who I would consider an experienced runner, decided that she'd encourage me during my training and fly in from Vancouver, B.C. and run the race with me. From what I'd read you could go from couch to 5K in about eight weeks. I had about twelve weeks so I was confident I could get in shape in time.

Not too long after my trip to New York we went through a reorganization at work, which meant that I got a new boss who would be based out of Chicago. In August, he was coming to town along with his boss, our new Regional Vice President, for our region meeting. Typically, when our senior leadership comes to town for big meetings it means I'll be working late. There's usually meetings all day followed by dinner. When my bosses aren't in town I typically don't work late away from home. If I need to work late I'll usually take work home with me. I let Jamal know that I'd be home late and he had his typical response. It always seems to me that he acts like I'm seeing someone on the side or partying. He gives me attitude and he can't just come home after work. Now he has to make sure he goes out and going out entails drinking. I got home around eight or nine o'clock and he wasn't home. I called his phone and texted him but received no answer. At that point I was upset because I wasn't going to sleep well since I'd be worried about him and I had to be at work early the next morning for day two of our meeting.

Over the years I'd seen a pattern developing and was becoming increasingly aware of the fact that the marriage is not going to work for me. In hindsight, I realized that I married Jamal because I didn't want to go through my cancer battle alone. I liked the feeling of love, familiarity, and we made a good team when we were on the same page. One of the things that attracted me to Jamal when we first met was the compassion he showed toward J.J. There's no shortage of black men who don't take care of healthy children and here he was stepping up to the plate with a disabled son. He's a great caregiver to his son so I'd thought he'd be a great caregiver to me. I'd always known Jamal to be a fighter and I thought that he would fight with me. I thought the fact that I had cancer would affect him differently. I thought he would rise to the occasion. I thought he would try harder. I believed that he wanted to make it work this time around and would give it his all. I was wrong. My cancer had very little effect on his behavior and he wasn't making any effort to make the marriage work.

Ending this marriage had always been in the back of my mind. I'd told Jamal just days before that I was leaving because of his drinking and his bad attitude and now this. I know I'd have left sooner if I had family in the area or money to fall back on but I didn't.

Finally, around two in the morning I got a call from Jamal's mother saying that he was in jail. After leaving a bar, he hit a tree coming off the exit to our house and totaled his Range Rover. Supposedly, he tried to call me but I didn't answer, which I highly doubted. For one thing, my phone didn't ring and, another, he knows I would have hung up on him so he wouldn't have called me. He needed $500 dollars to post bail but he couldn't get out until eight in the morning. He also wanted to try to make it to work on time so they wouldn't get wind of what had happened. This was the last straw for me. Another drinking incident and he technically didn't have a license still so he shouldn't have been driving anyway. But he didn't listen to me when I'd advised him not to. He's so hardheaded! I was not about to jeopardize my job to bail him out of jail. I was nice enough to take a check and a change of clothes to his mother's house at five in the morning and then proceeded to make it to my meeting on time as if nothing had happened.

According to Jamal this was perceived by his mother as being insensitive but I wasn't about to let his poor judgment interfere with my career and the impression I was making at work. Had he been in a true accident of course I would have been there for him. If he'd been in jail for fighting for civil rights or something honorable I'd have been there to bail him out with a sign that said "Free Jamal." But this was once again something that happened because of the poor choices that he'd made. He needed a "ride or die" chick and that wasn't me. I felt like he was going to bring me down if I didn't end it. He wasn't an asset to me. He was more of a liability and I was smarter than this. I just needed to get all of my ducks in a row and I would move out.

I'd been doing fine with my 5K training until Jamal's accident. I learned that running is very mental and my mind just wasn't into it. I'd worked up to running twenty minutes without stopping but that wasn't going to get me through the entire race. I was going to have to rely on Cynthia to get me through. One of the girls at work, Skyler, had also joined my team so the three of us would run together. My office had a team as well. The night before the race Cynthia and I stayed in San Francisco near Embarcadero where the race would take place. The other breast cancer walks I'd participated in followed the same trail but I'd always walked. This time I was running.

Cynthia and Skyler were so sweet to stay with me and encourage me. They both had run at least half marathons and I was running so slow that a lady next to me, who also took to encouraging me, was walking and keeping pace with me. I didn't run the whole race but Cynthia said I walked very little. They took my picture crossing the finish line and there was another survivor eating my dust so I'm pretty proud of that.

I felt bad that Cynthia didn't really get the experience she was used to or expecting when hanging out with me. Since Jamal didn't have a car or driver's license I'd been driving him back and forth between Stockton and Oakland where he worked—almost an hour and a half drive one-way. Most of Cynthia's and my time was spent in the car commuting. We did manage to do a drive-by wine pairing at Kendall Jackson winery in Sonoma, which was beautiful and scrumptious. But if we'd had our druthers we'd have stayed the night or spent more time meandering through the town, shopping, and winetasting.

Soon after the race my Gatorade bottles hit the shelves. It would've been cool to have them at the race but the timing didn't work out. Unfortunately, the bottles weren't sold in Northern California so I didn't get to see them in my grocery stores but friends and colleagues were buying them and sending me pictures of them in stores in other parts of the country. My job ordered me a bunch of cases for souvenirs. It was a lot of fun. I signed a few bottles like I was some sort of rock star. The bottles were sold in the Dallas area so my family got a kick out of seeing displays of my bottles and telling people that I was related to them.

October was a good month. I always celebrate another year being cancer-free, I had my face on a Gatorade bottle, and I got a promotion. I was assistant category manager and our category manager had decided to leave the company shortly after returning from maternity leave. I'd been doing her job while she was out so I asked to be considered for her job and I got it. Now I'd have a company car and be bonus eligible. It was a very exciting time.

The next month at work, our senior leadership came to town again. This time it wasn't a big meeting but we would have a team dinner. Jamal and I were commuting so I let him know that

I had a dinner and that he could just keep himself busy with his friends until I was done. I dropped him off at one of their favorite spots and I went to my dinner, which wasn't far from where he was. When I got to my restaurant I let him know where I was just so he wouldn't show up there. His friends were quite the socialites in town and knew just about every restaurateur, restaurant manager, and bartender. I knew it was highly likely that they could end up in the same place as my dinner.

We had dinner in a private room. There were about twenty of us. I sat in the middle of the long table facing the window that looked out to the front of the restaurant. My boss and his boss sat at one end. I'd been trying to adhere to a vegan diet for a couple of months, so I asked the waiter if they had anything vegan on the menu. He said he would ask the chef to prepare something for me. When the servers brought out our food I had a red pepper stuffed with couscous and vegetables. It was very tasty. A little later the chef came out and asked me how I liked my meal. I was flattered that he gave me special attention. I told him it tasted great and thanked him for preparing a dish just for me. He told me it was his pleasure. Then he said to me, "Your husband is here with Steve and the gang." Jamal's friend, Steve, is a very nice, professional family man but he can really drink. So can the rest of Jamal's friends-- birds of a feather. Steve was friends with the chef. I looked out the door and saw Jamal at the bar with his boys. I looked back at the chef and said, "Tell him to go away. I'm sure they've been drinking." The chef said, "Steve drinking? Noooo" and laughed.

The chef left and I ignored the fact that my husband and his boys were in the bar outside of my business dinner. Things could get ugly so I wasn't going out there. The chef came back again and said "Jamal said that you have his credit card". My co-worker overheard the chef and said, "Oh, your husband's here?! You should go and say hi." I was quite perturbed at this point. I took my purse and went out to the bar. It was a very small restaurant and you had to go through the bar to get to the restroom. I was hoping no one would have to relieve themselves and see me out in the bar with my husband and his buddies who had been drinking. Jamal was seething. He said he'd been trying to call me because I had his credit card. He and his friends were going to a nearby city to party but he needed his card. I had gone to the bank for him earlier and forgotten to give it back to him. He was pissed because, I'm sure, when I didn't answer my phone he didn't really think I was having a business dinner. Since he'd seen I was having a business dinner but didn't answer my phone or come out he thought I was embarrassed by him and wanted to make a good impression for "the man."

The reason I didn't answer my phone was because I was at a business dinner and my phone was in my purse. He knew I was at a business dinner and I figured he wouldn't disturb me unless it was a true emergency, not because he needed his credit card. One of his boys could have spotted him. Since he was there I was nervous because I knew I had dropped him off at a bar and although he said he didn't have anything to drink I wasn't stupid. A whole hour had passed since I'd dropped him off. Usually his first two drinks were thirst quenchers so I was sure he'd had a few drinks and now was at my business dinner.

He was giving me serious attitude. I clearly didn't want to cause a scene. I hugged all of his friends, give Jamal his credit card, and returned to my dinner. I was sitting at the table and out the window I saw the chef with his arm around the guys walking them to their car laughing and having a good ole time. There were about five of them total. I called that a scene and I was so livid! Once again Jamal showed his ass while I was working late. Luckily, no one from my work realized what was going on. I didn't find out if Jamal needed a ride home after dinner. I just left. He had his credit card and could get a room. I was done.

I spent the holidays in Dallas with my family. This was a precursor of things to come. I decided things were going to be different in 2012. In 2012, I wouldn't be going through the same things I'd been going through over the last few years. I was moving out and moving on. Some things had changed from my first marriage with Jamal, but a lot had stayed the same. I felt as though I didn't need to spend a lot of time trying to work things out. This was the second, and last, chance.

Dr. Scott had warned me about keeping my stress down to avoid recurrence. Jamal just didn't seem to understand how his choices were affecting my life. He figured if he was drinking in the comfort of his home it shouldn't be a problem. If he totaled his car and had to go to jail, why was I the one stressed out? He was the one who might go to jail. He acted like my driving him around was my duty as a wife. If I made the haul from Stockton to Oakland again I just might snap. He just didn't get it and I didn't want him to be the death of me.

It was like old times spending the holidays with my family. I hadn't spent the holidays with them in a while. We rang in the New Year quietly at home and that was just fine with me.

Karla at the Gatorade Photo Shoot with Makeup Artist,
Margina Dennis and Hair Stylist, Ianthe Foushée |
New York, NY

Survivorship: Year Five

CHAPTER EIGHTEEN:
Cured

"My mission in life is not merely to survive, but to thrive; and to do so with some passion, some compassion, some humor, and some style."

-- Maya Angelou

Two thousand twelve was the year I'd been looking forward to. This was the year that I could officially consider myself cured because I'd have been cancer-free for five years. Not only had I not had a recurrence, I was alive and could say I was on the right side of the five year survival statistics. I really planned to celebrate this milestone to the fullest. I wanted to surround myself with positivity and peace. Nothing would take me out of the space of gratitude I'd be in throughout the year. It truly was the year I'd been longing to reach.

My first order of business was getting my own place. I finally got my proverbial ducks in a row in March and got an apartment in Oakland's Jack London Square. Jamal and I were still friends though. Since my apartment was in Oakland and Jamal worked in Oakland we would still get together for dinner and cocktails or sometimes he'd stay the night if he missed his train home. This split wasn't nearly as difficult emotionally as the first one. Neither of us took the separation hard. I'd been saying I was leaving for a few months and since we'd divorced before Jamal knew I was serious. I don't think he was interested in doing the things it took to be a better husband so he didn't stand in my way.

My apartment was perfect because it was on the estuary, dog friendly, and you could walk to nearby restaurants. I worked from home quite a bit, but when I needed to go into the office it was a short drive going opposite to the commuters heading to San Francisco. The apartment complex had a little grassy area overlooking the water where all the dog owners would meet and let their dogs play. I was concerned about Armani adjusting to city life but he quickly caught on to his timed outings. He looked forward to his after work playdates with the neighbors' dogs. His inner clock would alert him to look out the window right around five o'clock. Every Friday we had a doggie happy hour after work. The doggie parents from around the area would BYOB and let the dogs run around off leash. I dubbed Armani "the Mayor" since he liked running up to every dog to greet them as if every dog wanted to be his friend. Sometimes he got a rude awakening.

Not long after settling in to my new digs I decided to get out of my comfort zone a little bit. Twenty twelve was election year and the Republicans' main objectives were to deny President Obama a second term and repeal the Affordable Care Act. Unlike with the last election, I was healthy so I wanted to be more involved than I'd been in 2008 when I'd been going through treatment. Although I hadn't been in Oakland long, I decided to run to be a delegate at the Democratic National

Convention. I wanted to stand with California during the roll call as they boasted about all the great attributes the state possessed and cast our vote to re-nominate President Obama as our presidential candidate. I thought my chances were slim since I was a newcomer to the district but it was worth a try. Life is too short to have regrets. If I didn't try I'd always wonder how things could have turned out so I went for it. I linked up with my local Organizing for America office to make connections and also to sign up to be a volunteer for the presidential campaign. I posted flyers everywhere I could and even attended a democratic club meeting, which exposed me to a totally new world that I hadn't known existed. The particular night that I attended the club the members were analyzing one of President Obama's speeches and discussing the points that he made. These people were very passionate about their politics. I could tell some of them could go on for hours if you let them. I also got one of my politically conscious co-workers to bar hop with me in downtown Oakland to leave behind some of my flyers. A couple of my other colleagues even joined me on caucus day to help pass them out. The experience was a lot of fun but in the end I didn't win. Nonetheless, everyone at the caucus was very surprised by how well I did considering I'd only been in the district a short time. I got more votes than some people who'd been in the district much longer.

The caucus happened in spring. By summer some interesting things started to happen. For some reason my taste had changed and I started to drink a lot more champagne. I collected corks, something I'd started doing when I was in Paris. I have tons of them from special dinners with friends at my place, dinners at restaurants, vacations, or sometimes just a good bottle that I wanted to remember. I always keep corks unless they're the cheap plastic ones. Typically, I have a lot of wine corks but I realized I was hardly collecting wine corks anymore. I mostly had champagne corks. I think I was in celebration mode and I didn't even realize it. Champagne had become my drink of choice. It became a staple at my place. I love to hear the popping of the cork. It made me feel happy and it just dawned on me, when I looked at the decorative wine barrel that I keep my corks in, that my subconscious had already gotten the "Karla's Cured" party started.

There was something else that my inner self led me to do. Cry. Out of the blue. It was a beautiful day and I was in my living room talking on the phone with my sister, Brianna. We were just talking about nothing in particular and I had the sudden urge to cry. It was so bizarre. I said, "I feel like I want to cry but I'm not sad or depressed. I'm happy." She said, "Well go with. It might be good for you." When we got off of the phone, I sat there with my eyes closed and asked myself, *Why would you want to cry?* I thought of how blessed I was and all that God had brought me through over the last five years. Boy, did the tears start flowing. I cried the "ugly cry" from my belly. I shed tears that I'd probably held in for five years except these tears weren't tears of sadness. They were tears of relief. I bawled like I'd just made it through the toughest battle of my life unscathed and I had. When I really thought about it, I realized you couldn't cry and fight at the same time. It made me think of a child who is crying uncontrollably out of anger or frustration because maybe you took their favorite toy. They typically stop crying when they try to hit you. That is what happened to me. I hadn't cried much before because I was in the middle of the fight. It wasn't until my body felt I was in the clear that I had this urge to let it go. My official cure date was still a couple of months out but my body knew that the battle was over.

When I saw Dr. Scott in August I told her that I supposed we could say I was cured, since if the cancer came back it wouldn't kill me by September or October. She laughed. She said that the day I was diagnosed (in September) is technically my survivor anniversary but I like to celebrate it in October when the cancer was removed from my body. That's when I consider myself to have been cancer-free and a survivor.

My last quarterly visit with Dr. Scott wasn't due until November but I timed it to be in October since it was such a milestone for me. I asked Dr. Scott not to examine me in the room where she first examined me because I thought I might cry. However, I did want a picture with her in that room. I felt I could handle that. To me the room was symbolic of how far I'd come. It was the room where she'd given me that look that had made me cry five years before. It was the room where my dad had told me we would beat this. It was the room where Dr. Scott had told me that she thought I was curable and thanks be to God she was right.

Before I left there was one question that I wanted Dr. Scott to answer for me. "What does it really mean to be cured? I know it doesn't mean that my cancer can't or won't come back so why do we say I'm cured?" I asked. I'd heard of people having recurrences after ten years or more so I was confused about what "cured" really meant. She said, "What it officially means is that your risk of recurrence is lower. Typically, the first three years is the highest risk of recurrence. Five years is when we consider a patient clinically cured, but it doesn't mean that your cancer can't come back. It is just less likely that it will." At any rate, I was rolling with it. I was cured and that's what you'll hear me say. Like I said before I won't say I'm in remission because I think it sounds like I expect that shit to come back. It may sound like semantics but I choose to say that I'm cured!

That visit with Dr. Scott in early October set the ball rolling.

October was a busy month for me in more ways than one. Dr. Scott asked me to be in her practice's Surviving In Style fashion show, which was so much fun. The following week I flew to Seattle to celebrate being cured with my longtime girlfriends. I had decided to have two celebrations—one in Seattle with friends and one in Dallas with my family.

For the Seattle celebration I got the idea to have a pole dancing party. I was going to be single again and would need to get my sexy back so what better way to do that than to learn to work a pole? I called it "Karla's Cured Pole Dancing Extravaganza." I invited seven of my girlfriends. I bought all of us pink boas and I even went to a sex shop and got myself some clear, platform heels like strippers wear. We all chose stripper names so that we could get into character. I was Champagne since I'd been drinking so much of it. I was joined by Bunni, Tutti, Coco, Peaches, Diamond, Foxy, and Kandi. We sounded like exotic dancers from a first rate strip club but we sure didn't look like it. None of us could quit our day jobs. Pole dancing is a lot of fun but it sure is a workout. You gotta hand it to those professional pole dancers. They're in great shape to do the things they do. They earn every penny they get. It was hard trying to slink around while also trying not to fall on your face wearing those super high platform heels. We had a blast though!

Cancer wasn't the only thing I was cured of and could celebrate in Seattle. I was also cured of my sex drought. I hadn't had sex in a very long time. Jamal and I had stopped having sex long before I'd moved out and when we were having sex it was business as usual. Jamal didn't seem turned on by me at all until he was drunk and when he was drunk I was turned off. I could walk around the house butt naked and he would be unfazed. I don't think my breasts had anything to do with it though. He never seemed bothered by them. He's a booty man. I just think we had so much emotional baggage that sex with each other was the furthest thing from our minds. Even though Jamal wasn't turned on by me and I only had one good breast, I knew deep down inside that I was still sexy. I just needed someone to draw it out. My soul was longing for a lover who would look at me with lust in his eyes.

I had an ex-lover in Seattle who always loved my body and made me feel beautiful. We could never make a relationship work for one reason or another but we had great chemistry. I'd heard that he'd asked my girlfriends about me when he'd found out that I had had cancer but he didn't reach out because he knew that I had remarried Jamal. Since I was going to be in town I decided to contact him to see how he was doing. He was happy to hear from me and to learn that I was doing well and was separated. We made plans to see each other. It was a given that we were going to have sex. We could never keep our hands off of each other.

At first, I was a little apprehensive about being naked in front of him. He'd always taken very good care of his body. I'd gained a lot of weight since he'd seen me last and now I had my breast issues. I wasn't sure how he'd handle it since he'd liked my body so much before. I decided to tell him what to expect before I saw him.

"You know that I had breast cancer so...I had my breast removed but...my breast isn't fully reconstructed yet." I explained. "So I'll probably keep my top on when we make love."

"Why? When I make love to you, I want to make love to *all* of you."

After hearing that I knew I was in for a treat. He did indeed make love to *all* of me and not for a few minutes but a few hours. He caressed and kissed my affected breast just like it was a real one and he still loved my body even with the extra weight. I think he liked me even more heavy since most of the weight had gone to my butt. Yep, he was a booty man too.

The fling was good for me and my self-esteem. It let me know that the right man wouldn't have a problem with my breast. It would take a pretty shallow man to not be able to look past it. If I met a man who couldn't, I wouldn't want to date him anyway.

From the "Karla's Cured" party in Seattle I flew to Dallas to celebrate with family. My visit coincided with the exact date of the anniversary of my mastectomy, so we were able to celebrate my being cured and Teressa's forty-fifth birthday. My dad had moved to Dallas to reunite with my mom a few months prior to my trip. Although I was hoping to celebrate with my parents, my party got a little derailed because they had to make a last minute trip to Seattle a few days prior and weren't able to make it back in town in time for dinner. Teressa, our Godsister who flew in from Seattle, and I got dressed up and went out to dinner. It wasn't as big a production as Seattle but it was nice to be able to celebrate being cured with my family.

Election Day followed less than two weeks after my trip to Dallas. President Obama was in Chicago (his hometown) to vote and celebrate should he win. As luck would have it, I was in Chicago as well on business. When I found out that I'd be in town I'd wished that I could get into the Election Night celebration at McCormick Place convention center but I thought it was a tall order. I didn't want to sit in my hotel room though and watch the votes roll in via television so I volunteered to phone bank at the local Organizing for America office. I wanted to be with other supporters and in the middle of the action.

The campaign office was abuzz. You could sense the expectation of victory in the air. I only made a few phone calls before the election was called for President Obama. He was officially a two-term president and the Affordable Care Act would remain intact. To thank us for our service, volunteers were given passes or "credentials" to attend the Election Night celebration. Although I came to the campaign office alone I didn't attend the celebration alone. A tall, dark, and handsome volunteer by the name of Lance took me to a jazz lounge for a few drinks and then on to McCormick Place. I don't usually go off with strangers but we hit it off and he was there volunteering with his mother. How sweet! I figured he couldn't be an axe murderer. At first, I wasn't physically attracted to Lance. He was bundled up in a puffy coat, beanie, and a hoody since he'd been out door knocking. He looked kind of thuggish to me. But, when he picked me up at my hotel in his Jaguar wearing jeans, a t-shirt, and a blazer, he looked totally different. Not only was he handsome, he had a nice body too! Score! I really enjoyed his company. We had a lot of fun together at the convention center dancing, people watching, and taking pictures. Being at the celebration was such a privilege. A once in a lifetime experience. It was a nice consolation for having lost the delegation caucus in the spring.

Since I go to Chicago often on business Lance and I keep in touch. He has absolutely no problem with my breast.

I realize how blessed I am to have made it as far as I have. There are so many women who weren't as fortunate as me. Not a day goes by that I don't think about cancer. How can I forget? I have so many reminders—my partially reconstructed breast, my port scar, my medications, my hot flashes. But not only do those things remind me of cancer. They also remind me to live life to the fullest. People die every day without warning. No chance to tell their loved ones they love them. No opportunity to have one last kiss or enjoy one last sunrise or sunset. I've been given the gift of time. With this gift I plan to live and not die. Just like you can't un-ring a bell, I can't go back to the time when I took life for granted and thought I was entitled to a perfect life. Every life will have some rain. The question isn't if the rain will fall but how will you react when it does. I dug in my heels which is the same as dropping your anchor if you're in a boat during a storm and you don't want to be tossed to and fro. I'm grateful that I had a spiritual foundation in my life to draw upon and a relationship with God. He and His word were and are my anchor.

I'm happy that cancer has gotten smaller and smaller in my rearview mirror. There's so much that I'm looking forward to. My "FORTY, Cancer-FREE, and FABULOUS" party will be held in Maui. I'm getting lei'd for the first time! Hawaii was always on my list of places to visit but after I fell in love with Paris it took a back seat to trips to Europe. Now that I've lived in Paris I can see some other places. I'm so eager to be on the beach and get some much needed rest and relaxation. I can't wait to hear the pop of a champagne bottle opening and toast to being alive to see my big 4-0.

Afterword

"We spend precious hours fearing the inevi-
table. It would be wise to use that time adoring
our families, cherishing our friends and living
our lives."

– Maya Angelou

After almost seven years of being cancer-free, my breast cancer returned and spread to my spine which made it stage IV. Doctors say that someone in my condition can live for several years, which is encouraging. When I first got the news, I was afraid. I'd always looked at stage IV cancer as the beginning of the end. But after a couple of weeks of being fearful, I decided enough was enough. I didn't like how it felt. If I could live for several years, how long was I going to be afraid? Living in fear was not how I wanted to spend my life however long it was going to be. I recalled a scripture that reads, "For God has not given us a spirit of fear, but of power and of love and of a sound mind."[3] I told the fear to go back to the pit of hell from whence it came and I made room for power, love, and a sound mind. That's truly what I have now—power, love, and a sound mind. If you're defeated and fraught with fear by the news of a cancer diagnosis you've already done part of cancer's job which is to make your body stressed and depressed enough that it doesn't heal. Instead of fear, I chose to have faith—faith in knowing that God is bigger than cancer. Everyone calls cancer "the big C" and we've become so afraid of it. Well, I call Christ "the big C" and cancer "the little c." I take comfort in knowing that God is always in control. My life will be what He wants it to be. My job is to tap into the Holy Spirit to learn and understand what my part is in receiving my healing--whether it's prayer, meditation, exercise, diet, or stillness--and to keep pursuing my goals and fulfilling my purpose.

I chose to be treated at the Cancer Treatment Centers of America (CTCA) because of their integrative approach to care. They are the only place that I knew of that would treat my mind, body, and spirit. I didn't want to just treat this cancer with surgery, drugs and radiation. I wanted to use food and supplements to manage any side effects I might have and to build my immune system as well. The good news is I don't have to have chemo or radiation, which is a testament to how far we've come with cancer treatment. I take medication that reduces my estrogen since my cancer was estrogen fed. I was forced back into menopause, so those damn hot flashes are back. But, hot flashes are very mild compared to what I could be faced with. I'm very grateful and I'm pleased with the care that CTCA is providing me. I WAS DIAGNOSED IN JULY OF 2014 AND I'VE BEEN CANCER-FREE SINCE FEBRUARY OF 2015. I don't think I would have had the same results as quickly anywhere else. I

---

3   2 Tim. 1:7 (New King James Version)

see how my diet, nutrition, and exercise have played a part in how well I feel.

This cancer battle has been very different than the first one. For one, I was fortunate enough to move to Dallas to be closer to my family just a few months prior to my recurrence. I have the same job but since I cover the Texas market it was okay for me to relocate. Secondly, I'm divorced and there's less negativity in my life. Lastly, I'm much wiser about my health this time around. I'm eating right, working out on a regular basis and my weight is in the normal range again. It's unfortunate that it took a recurrence to make me do the things that I should've been doing anyway but the results have been amazing. I look and feel great! This recurrence really is bringing me to my best self. There's a saying, "Never place a period where God has placed a comma." I believe this recurrence is a comma and the best is still yet to come.

There was a question that I asked myself when I was first diagnosed with cancer: Do people die before they've fulfilled their purpose? My personal belief now is that we all die with potential but we don't die not having fulfilled our purpose. Every person who dies could have done more had it not been for death. However, we'll all die when we have served our purpose. Some of our purposes are long assignments. Some of them are shorter. Some of us may touch a lot of people. Some of us will touch a few. My mantra is "One life to live, many lives to touch." I believe I have many days ahead of me and my work has just begun.

Breast Health Tips

Since I have you held captive, I want to share some key information about breast health. I'm not a doctor and the information here shouldn't substitute for the advice of a medical professional. It's for educational purposes only.

Early Detection

I'm sure you've heard it before but early detection is key. It saves lives and breasts. Although a lot of women know this to be true, they're still scared to do breast self-exams and/or get mammograms. I think they'd rather not know if something is wrong. However, if there's something wrong, not knowing isn't going to change it. It will just allow it to get worse. You have a better chance of surviving beyond five years if you catch breast cancer before it spreads outside of the breasts. The earlier you catch it, the less aggressively you might be able to treat it, which means you could avoid chemotherapy and/or radiation and you might be able to spare your breasts.

Breast Self-Exams

I used to hate doing breast self-exams. I did them but they made me feel like I was expecting something to show up in my breasts every month. Now I know that it's just a way for us to become familiar with our breasts and to understand what normal feels like. That way, when something changes, we pick up on it early.

Although experts no longer recommend breast self-exams as a screening tool for breast cancer, I still believe they are necessary, especially for women under forty who aren't old enough to have their mammograms covered by insurance. I know women who found their breast cancer between their annual mammograms. If they hadn't been doing breast self-exams, they wouldn't have found the cancer when they did. And of course you know my story so it's safe to say that I'm an advocate for breast self-exams.

But, I take the typical breast self-exam and add another step to it. After you have walked your fingers across every inch of your breasts, take the time to squeeze them too. As you read, my lump wasn't detectable when doing the typical breast self-exam, but it could be felt when I squeezed. There are instances when husbands have found their wives' lumps and you can believe they weren't walking their fingers over their wives' breasts. So go ahead and give your breasts a good squeeze.

If you notice any of these symptoms when you are examining your breasts, please see your doctor:

- Swelling of part or all of the breast
- Nipple discharge
- An inverted nipple
- Unusual breast or nipple pain
- Skin irritation or dimpling
- Redness, scaling, or thickening of the nipple or breast
- Swelling of the underarm

• Breast feeling warmer than usual

There are some benign (non-cancerous) conditions of the breast that can cause similar symptoms so it's important to see your doctor if you notice these symptoms. But don't panic. It may not be cancer.

Clinical Breast Exams

A clinical breast exam is simply a breast exam performed by a medical professional. Experts recommend that these should be done every three years if you are under forty and every year if you are forty and older. I'd say all women should have their doctors examine their breasts when they go in for their annual pap smear. I don't think anything concerning your health should be done every three years.

Mammograms

Unless you have a high risk of developing breast cancer, you should start having annual mammograms at age forty. Don't skip a mammogram because it can help you find breast cancer at an earlier stage, before it can be felt or picked up by a breast self-exam. If you catch breast cancer before it can be felt or when the lump is small, you might be able to save your breast(s) and avoid having a mastectomy.

Mammograms don't hurt. They may be a little uncomfortable but they aren't painful. I haven't breastfed a baby but, from what I've seen, that would be more painful than a mammogram so don't let the thought that it might hurt stop you from getting one.

Dense Breasts

Dense breasts have less fatty tissue and more fibrous and glandular tissue than breasts that are not dense and may slightly increase your risk of getting breast cancer. Dense breasts make it hard to detect breast cancer on mammograms. If you have dense breasts, talk to your doctor about having a breast MRI, ultrasound or tomosynthesis (3D mammography). "How do I know if I have dense breasts?" you may ask. When you have your mammogram and the doctor shares the results with you, ask the question "Do I have dense breasts?" Or if you receive the results via mail, it might be in the letter so read the letter carefully. If you haven't received your results in a reasonable amount of time, follow-up with the office. No news is not always good news. You could have fallen through the cracks so you need to make certain everything is okay.

Twenty one states have enacted breast density notification laws that require physicians to notify you if you have dense breasts. You can go to www.areyoudenseadvocacy.org to find out if your state is one of them.

Breast Cancer Risk

The following factors can have an impact on your risk of developing breast cancer. I call these the uncontrollables.

- Age when you started your menstrual cycle. Women who menstruated before the age of twelve have a higher risk of developing breast cancer.
- Age when you had your first child. Women who gave birth at age thirty-five or younger have a lower risk.

- Number of children you have. The more children you give birth to, the lower your risk.
- Age at menopause. Going into menopause at an early age decreases your risk.
- Family history of breast cancer. A woman with a first degree relative (mother, sister, or daughter) who has had breast cancer has almost twice the risk of developing breast cancer.
- Genetics. If you have any of the known breast cancer gene mutations (BRCA1, BRCA2, p53, CHEK2, ATM, PALB2), you are at an increased risk of developing breast cancer. If you have a family history of breast cancer you may want to consider genetic testing.
- Breast density. Women with dense breast are at a higher risk of developing breast cancer.
- Treatment with radiation to the breast/chest. Exposure to radiation can increase your risk of cancer.

Ways to reduce your risk of developing breast cancer (the controllables):

- Maintain a healthy weight. Women who are overweight or obese have a higher risk.
- Exercise. Seventy five to one hundred and fifty minutes of brisk walking each week has been shown to lower breast cancer risk.
- Don't smoke. Smoking is linked to a higher risk of breast cancer.
- Limit alcohol. Having two or more alcoholic beverages a day increases your risk of developing breast cancer.
- Avoid hormone replacement therapy (HRT). Taking replacement hormones is linked to a higher risk of breast cancer.

- Vitamin D. Women with lower levels of vitamin D have a higher risk of breast cancer. Your doctor can check your levels with a simple blood test.

Types of Breast Cancer

Invasive Ductal Carcinoma

The most common type of breast cancer is invasive or infiltrating ductal carcinoma (IDC). IDC is just what it sounds like—breast cancer that originated in the milk duct and is invading or spreading through the wall of the duct and into the breast tissue. Once breast cancer has spread into the breast tissue, it can spread (metastasize) through the lymphatic system or blood stream to other parts of the body. This is why mammograms are so important. In most cases, a mammogram would be able to detect breast cancer before it spreads outside of the duct and before you can detect it with your fingers.

Invasive Lobular Carcinoma

The second most common type of breast cancer is invasive or infiltrating lobular carcinoma (ILC). ILC starts in the lobules or milk producing glands but spreads outside of the lobule into surrounding areas. ILC can be more difficult to detect by mammogram than IDC.

Ductal Carcinoma In Situ

Ductal carcinoma in situ (DCIS) is also referred to as Intraductal Carcinoma. In Situ means "In place." DCIS is contained in the duct and is considered non-invasive, pre-invasive, or pre-cancerous. If you have breast cancer, this is the stage at which you want to catch it. DCIS is classified as stage 0 but if left untreated some (but not all) cases can progress into higher stages. The American Cancer Society shows the five year survival rate of stage 0 breast cancer to be one 100%. At this stage the question is less about if you will live and more about what type of treatment you will have.

Inflammatory Breast Cancer

Inflammatory breast cancer (IBC) is a rare but aggressive breast cancer that in its early stages is frequently misdiagnosed as a breast infection. With IBC cancer cells block lymph vessels in the skin of the breasts making the breasts inflamed. There may not be a palpable lump with IBC so it may not show up on a mammogram. This is why it's important to pay attention to changes in the appearance of your breasts such as dimpling, rashes, inflammation, heaviness, etc. and report them to your doctor. IBC has a higher chance of spreading and a worse prognosis or outlook than IDC or ILC so if you notice any changes in your breasts that point to IBC don't delay in getting in to see your doctor.

Other Types of Breast Cancer

There are other types of breast cancer but they're all detected in the same way—look at your breasts for changes in appearance, touch them to determine changes in how they feel, and get your mammograms, ultrasounds, and MRIs, if necessary. For more information on types of breast cancers you can go to the websites in the resources section of this book.

Characteristics of Breast Cancer

If you are diagnosed with breast cancer, your doctor should test the tumor for biomarkers. Biomarkers tell doctors how breast cancer behaves. Knowing how your cancer behaves will be key in determining how to treat it beyond the typical treatment options (surgery, radiation, and chemotherapy). Biomarkers are grouped based on the presence of estrogen receptors (ER) or progesterone receptors (PR) and whether or not there is an excess of the protein called HER2.

Classification Based on Biomarkers

- Hormone Receptor Positive: Breast cancers with hormone receptors use estrogen and/or progesterone to fuel their growth. The majority of breast cancers test positive for hormone receptors. To combat these types of breast cancers, your doctor would put you on hormone therapy that would consist of reducing the estrogen produced by your body and/or blocking the receptors from using hormones to flourish.
- Hormone Receptor Negative: Breast cancers that are hormone receptor negative do not respond to hormone therapy. However, they may respond better to chemotherapy than hormone receptor positive breast cancers. Hormone receptor negative breast cancers are more common in women who are premenopausal.
- HER2 positive: Breast cancers that have an excess of HER2 protein tend to grow and spread aggressively. Treatment consists of drugs that target HER2.
- HER2 negative: These breast cancers don't have an excess of HER2 and don't respond well to treatment with drugs that target HER2.
- Triple Negative: If breast cancers are estrogen and progesterone receptor negative and HER2 negative they are called triple negative. Triple negative breast cancers are more common in younger women and African American

and Hispanic women. They tend to grow and spread quickly. Treatment options are limited for triple negative breast cancers because they don't respond to hormone therapy or drugs that target HER2.

- Triple Positive: Breast cancers that are estrogen and pro-gesterone positive and have an excess of HER2 are called triple positive. These types of cancers can be treated with hormone therapy and drugs that target HER2.

Staging and Five Year Survival Rates

There are four stages of breast cancer that are determined based on the size of the tumor, how many lymph nodes are affected, and whether or not the cancer has metastasized or spread beyond the breast and/or lymph nodes. The following stages and five year survival rates come from the National Cancer Institute's SEER database.

- Stage 0: Breast cancer that is "In Situ" or hasn't spread beyond its original place. Stage 0 has a 100% five year survival rate.
- Stage I, II, and III: Invasive breast cancers that haven't spread outside of the breast or lymph nodes. As the stages progress, tumor size increases as well as number of lymph nodes involved, and/or the size of the cancer in the nodes. It's also possible to have no tumor at all with lymph node involvement. Five year survival rates are 100% for Stage I, 93% for Stage II, and 72% for Stage III.
- Stage IV: Metastatic breast cancer, or breast cancer that has spread beyond the breast and/or lymph nodes into other parts of the body. The five year survival rate for Stage IV breast cancer is 22%.

Breast Cancer Disparities and African American Women

Breast cancer is the most common cancer among African American women. While African American women are less likely to be diagnosed with breast cancer than white women they're more likely to die from it. Additionally, African American women are diagnosed with breast cancer at an earlier age and a later stage than their white counterparts. Therefore, it's very important for African American to be cognizant of their breast cancer risk and stay on top of their breast health.

Online resources

The following resources were very helpful to me when I was battling breast cancer and while I was compiling this Breast Health Tips section. These sites provide a plethora of information about breast health.

- Cancer.org: The American Cancer Society offers a very comprehensive site that can be used by doctors, patients, caregivers, family, and friends. It has information on all types of cancers including information on their outreach programs that can assist you with getting a ride to treatment, joining a support group, or choosing a wig.
- Breastcancer.org: A comprehensive breast cancer resource with information surrounding breast cancer, treatment options, and day to day matters concerning living with breast cancer.
- ChemoCare.com: When I needed to understand the drugs I was prescribed for treatment, this is the site I went to. It has a list of cancer drugs, how they are administered, their side effects, and how to manage them.

- Dslrf.org: Dr. Susan Love Research Foundation. Dr. Susan Love literally wrote the book on breasts. I received her *Breast Book* from a fellow survivor shortly after I was diagnosed. It covers every aspect of your breasts and also covers breast cancer and cancer treatment. Her website is also a great resource.
- Komen.org: The Susan G Komen website is another great resource that's useful for patients, caregivers, friends, and family. You can use this site to learn more about breast cancer, life after treatment, and getting involved in races and other outreach programs.
- Cancer.gov: The National Cancer Institute website has educational information for patients as well as the latest information on cancer research.
- Nationalbreastcancer.org: The National Breast Cancer Foundation is a great resource for educating yourself on breast cancer and breast health. They also have breast health outreach programs and support services.
- Cancerandcareers.org: Cancer and Careers offers a comprehensive website, free publications, career coaching, and a series of educational seminars for employees with cancer and their health care providers and co-workers. If you are employed and have cancer or know someone who is, you should visit this site. The information Cancer and Careers provides is invaluable and I've not seen it offered elsewhere.
- Cancercenter.com: The Cancer Treatment Centers of America are phenomenal in their integrative approach to treating cancer. Visit their site to learn what makes them different and contact them for a second opinion.
- CDC.gov/cancer: Centers for Disease Control and Prevention (CDC) is a leader in nationwide efforts to

ease the burden of cancer. The CDC provides a wealth of information and resources, including downloadable fact sheets. They also offer free or low-cost mammograms to those who qualify.

- FDA.gov: The U.S. Food and Drug Administration (FDA) regulates the standards for mammography machines and training for the people who give mammograms. Under the Mammography Quality Standards Act (MQSA), the FDA certifies the places that give mammograms in the U.S and keeps a list of all certified places where you can get a mammogram. There is a searchable database on their website that allows you to find a certified site in your area. They also have great fact sheets and information on food and drug safety for consumers.
- Areyoudense.org: The Are You Dense? site is dedicated to the issue of dense breasts. If you have dense breasts or want to work to get dense breast notification legislation passed in your state, this is the site for you.

Acknowledgments

One hundred percent of the funds to publish this book came from the generous donations of my friends, family, co-workers, and strangers via crowdfunding on Kickstarter. Kickstarter was my Plan B. I'd always planned to self-publish my memoir and had saved the money, but once I had the recurrence I had to dip into my savings to pay for dental work that I needed to have before I could start treatment. As I mentioned before, I'd never been good at fundraising but I'd learned about Kickstarter and thought it could work. I was originally thinking that I needed to raise $5,000, but shortly before I launched the Kickstarter campaign, I was walking Armani and giving the campaign some thought. I realized that I really needed to set my goal at $10,000 if I wanted to net at least $5,000. I'd have to pay for donation rewards and Kickstarter fees with the money so a $5,000 goal wouldn't be enough.

When I returned to my apartment, I looked at my vision board, which has a mock-up of my book cover and I asked God how this was going to work. I thought $5,000 was a stretch, but now I realized I needed to raise $10,000. *How can I make this happen? I don't know enough people who would give me that kind of money.* I glanced over at my bookshelf and two books jumped out at me. The first was one of my favorite books, *Pour*

Your Heart Into It by Howard Schultz, founder of Starbucks. The second was *The Battle is the Lord's* by Tony Evans, a pastor of a mega church here in the Dallas area. I knew that was a message from God.

From that moment on, I knew I'd make my goal. I was supposed to pour my heart into the campaign and let God work out the details and that's what I did. I gave it my all and sat back to see how it would all come together. In addition to friends and family, I received donations from colleagues, some of whom I've never met. There were also some strangers who gave because of the relationship they have with the person who told them about the campaign. There are still a few backers who I have no idea who they are or how they found out about my campaign, which I think is pretty cool.

I'm truly grateful for the outpouring of love and support I received for this project. There were over 150 backers in total and I raised over $13,000! Below is a list of some of the major donors. While all of my backers are united around bringing awareness to breast cancer, they may not share my religious or political views. Therefore, a name listed below isn't an endorsement. Views expressed in this book are my own.

This book was made possible by the generous donations of Pennie Alston; Michaela N. & Gabriella Ambrose in Memory of Our Granny Beryl Adella Baptiste, M.B.E; Dr. Rosalind E. Ambrose, O.B.E and Mr. Dennis Ambrose, J.P. in Memory of Our Mom Beryl Adella Baptiste, M.B.E; Lindsey Avant; Daisy Axford; Bernard & Edna Baptiste in Memory of Dr. Wilbert & Sis. Johnnie Mae Reed and Ms. Neva Holland; Brianna Baptiste; Michelle Lynn Baptiste; Hon. Rene M Baptiste, C.M.G in Memory of My Mom Beryl Adella Baptiste, M.B.E; Kiara Baptiste-Taylor; Andrea Branch and Family in Memory of Joyce "Missy" Jones-Branch; Mrs. Margaret Britt; Veronica D. Cano;

Mildred Carter-Beaver in Memory of La Shana V. Johnson; Scott Cashman; Angela Davis-Lincoln in Memory of George Davis; Genise Dawson; Brielle Lynn Delaney; Yvette Deming; Athena Dunn; Jai-Anana Elliott; Deloris Gaines McGee; The Golden Voices Choir of the DeSoto Senior Center; Fabi R. Goncalves; Dayna Hailey in Memory of My Great Grandmother Fern Proctor; Jacqueline Hardy; Tye & Tress Heckler; Shevanne Helmer; New Walk Christian Church; Adina Hudrea; Carolyn Jackman; Rev. & Sis. S.B. Jackson; Nelda Jacobs; Paul Arthur Johnson CPA and Sali Gold-Johnson; Cortnie Kitzmiller; Denise LaBrie in Memory of Virginia Rogers; Treffaney R. Lowe; Jennifer Loyd; Trish Lukasik in Loving Memory of Art Evans; Denise McCarthy; Beverly Miller in Memory of Annette Stanton; Antoinette "Toni" Mitchell; Josephine Mitchell and All the Mitchell Women; Kevin Mizuta; Mary H. Murray in Memory of Wilbert T. Reed; New Mt. Zion Primitive Baptist Church; Michael Okech; Cynthia Palmer-Coleman in Memory of Ada Brooks; Tim Perry & Carlita Tohtz in Honor of Frances Perry and Joyce Perry; Jennifer C. Peters-Diamond, M.D., F.A.A.F.P in Memory of Ms. Joycie Edwards and Mrs. Sylvia Diamond; Crystal Phillips; Kyriah Porter; Taquitta Porter in Memory of Josephine Wright; Paul Rammer; P.A. Ratliff and Family in Memory of Norma Aaron; Yvette Russell in Memory of Waunema; Bobby Sango; Rozzy Shorter; Brooke M. Simmons; Emily Tan; Wendell & Teressa Taylor in Memory of Tisha Martin; Rev. Matthew & Sis. Nel Thornton in Memory of Nute & Clara B. Golidy and Rev. S.E. & Blanche E. Thornton; Andrea Trippe; Vay Vu; Leah Walker; Gina Washington in Memory of Lois Raymond; Cynthia Weathers; Didi Weber-Cowan; Dr. Fred West; Jonathan Williams; Victoria Wood; Kylee Young; Lisa Zagata; Joan Zetterlund and several other backers. Thank you for believing in me and this project.

I would also like to thank Dr. Rhoads for her contribution

to this book. She didn't hesitate at all when I asked her to write the foreword. I'm so grateful for her generous and humble spirit.

Pamela Ratliff, you are a precious gem. I'm so glad we connected at that Susan G Komen conference in San Francisco a few years back. Thank you for putting your eyes on this book, contributing to the breast health tips section, and always speaking encouraging words to me.

I'm also grateful to Chris Stewart of The Real Writer Editing Services for editing my manuscript and helping me bring my story to life. Chris, as a first time writer and publisher I'm grateful for your patience and experience.

Thank you Jessy J Photography and SASA Hair & Makeup for the beautiful job you did on my photos. I felt and looked like a star.

A big thank you to the Cancer Fighters team at the Cancer Treatment Centers of America – Midwestern Regional Medical Center. I appreciate you helping me spread the word about my book and allowing me to share my gifts and talents with the hospital.

I probably could go on and on but I would be remiss if I didn't thank my family. Thank you for being my proofreaders, consultants, marketing team, public relations specialists, prayer warriors, cheerleaders, and caregivers. You guys are the wind beneath my wings that has allowed me to soar. I love you with all my heart!

Readers Club Guide

1. The title of this book is *Dig In Your Heels*. How do you think the title ties into Karla's story?

2. What part of Karla's story could you relate to most?

3. Do you think Karla's feelings about her breasts had an impact on how she dealt with having to lose one of them? Why or why not?

4. Karla mentioned that she wasn't too concerned about losing her hair. How do you think you would deal with losing all of yours?

5. Karla wrote about wanting to be touched when she was going through treatment. How important do you think touch is to the healing process?

6. How much do you think Jamal's lack of intimacy affected Karla's self-esteem? Can you understand Karla's desire to find a lover who made her feel beautiful?

7. Do you think all of the support and encouragement that Karla received from friends, family, and strangers during treatment was instrumental in her healing process?

8. When Karla was healing from radiation she found comfort in her sister's dog, Fiona, which led her to get a dog of her own. Do you have a pet? Can you relate to Karla's experience with Fiona?

9. How much do you think spirituality played a role in Karla's approach to fighting cancer? How much do you think her attitude played a role in her reaching the five year cancer-free milestone?

10. Could you identify with Karla's aversion to crying while she was going through her cancer battle? Do you think she saw crying as a weakness?

11. After being diagnosed with cancer, Karla volunteered to help the Affordable Care Act become law. If you were diagnosed with a serious illness, would you give back and help others with your experience? If yes, how?

12. If you were faced with a terminal illness today, would you be able to say that you've followed your dreams like Karla did? What desires or passions have you left unfulfilled?

13. Has *Dig in Your Heels* inspired you in any way? If yes, how?

Follow Karla's Inspiring Journey

🌐 www.karlaliving.com

f www.facebook.com/KarlaABaptiste

🐦 @karlaliving

📷 @karlaliving

For all things *Dig in Your Heels* including photos that were not included in the book, go to www.diginyourheels.com

---

The bOOby Times

Karla publishes an online newspaper called *The bOOby Times* that is dedicated to the issue of (what else?) boobs. Let's face it. Breasts garner a lot of attention. There's boob related news every day from the latest in breast cancer research to celebrity nip slips. Subscribe to *The bOOby Times* today to stay abreast of the latest booby centric news. You are sure to find *The bOOby Times* an educational and entertaining read.

🌐 www.theboobytimes.com

f www.facebook.com/ThebOObyTimes

🐦 @theboobytimes

CPSIA information can be obtained
at www.ICGtesting.com
Printed in the USA
FSOW02n1727161015
12280FS

9 780578 169484